# Good Souls

# BAD SOULS

# and

# assholes

gratitude to you all for leaving your mark

# TINA THOMSON

*Dedication*

*Dedicated to my son Eric…*
*My life…*
*My everything.*

"This is more than a book and more than a random collection of stories; this is a manifesto of a renaissance woman who refused to allow any setback to handicap her destiny. She has the gumption, backbone, intellect, and a velvet chain saw to cut to the heart of the matter of any situation in a nanosecond. If you are lacking in fortitude, faith, and the favor of God, by the time you put this book down, you will have a fire lit within you that will burn out any doubt in yourself or anyone around you."

*Simon T. Bailey CEO of Simon T. Bailey International. Dedicated to teaching individuals and organisations how to be brilliant in an average world, Simon is the creator of the Shift Your Brilliance system and former Sales Leader of Disney.*

"'Stories have the power to heal, encourage, uplift and give hope'. Tina declares this while sharing her lifetime experiences full of love, hate, betrayal, entrepreneurial risks, heart-churning declarations, resilience, integrity and ethics. God-loving Tina with her unwavering faith talks of her struggles and joys in life. I salute her for all the achievements and especially for bringing up her very talented son Eric. Hats off to this precious lady who's made a huge impact on many and will keep on doing so because that's who she is! An awesome 'can't put it down' and 'lessons to learn from' book."

*Namita Krul-Taneja MBA, Financial Analyst, BNG Bank. Social Entrepreneur, Founder of New Yardsticks, Co-Founder of WORK+SHELTER*

"Tina inspires us by her capacity to overcome the intolerable. The depth of her boldness and courage are rare qualities. Like her, we have to be bold enough to take tough decisions in our life when needed. Tina's remarkable ability to share her deepest truth reminds us that only by being honest with ourselves can we ever be honest with others, no matter how uncomfortable honesty can be. Consequently, as is validated by Tina's life, truth leads to personal joy and inner peace. This book has been enlightening at many levels."

*Christine Asiko, Founder and CEO of Strive International.*

# Acknowledgements

**WRITING ONE'S MEMOIRS** is never easy. Thanking those who lived through the moments, days, weeks and years with me, and who made it possible to stay sane and to write the memoirs is much more difficult.

I know I have left out many precious memories and I have not shared many of my stories here. Forgive me. I'd like my family and friends to know that I have not forgotten a single one of our treasured moments. I may pen them at a later date? Mere words can never express how much I appreciate you. You have supported me through my life thus far and I know I can lean on you in the years to come.

Cousins Grace, Byron and Dianna – through my darkest of days, you gave me a home and you fed me. I am eternally grateful. Bless you!

My cherished brother - thank you for always encouraging me and for reminding me, through your own determination to **overcome**, and that we are part Spartan and part Ithacan; warriors and more than conquerors!

My beloved sister Selina, aka, Catie - thank you for your fervent prayers that sustain me, for keeping our family values and traditions alive and being loving, always. I appreciate your God-given talents.

A special note of thanks to my darling Ariel. Not only do you put a twinkle in my son's eyes, but you graciously offered to edit my book and painstakingly marked the manuscript and offered wise advice. With a sophistication way beyond your years, you amaze and delight me. Thank you Ariel.

My adored son, Eric - I can never communicate my appreciation and love enough. Thank you for your unconditional love and for being my reason to get out of bed each day, to thank God and to smile.

# Contents

# Foreword

**WOW...IS THE ONLY** word to describe such a passionate, real, and heart-wrenching book.

There are people who come through your life for a reason and a season, and then there are people who come into your life for a definite purpose. Tina Thomson has been a friend and colleague of mine for more than a decade, and I can honestly say that I am a better man, thinker, and business leader because of her brilliance.

I started reading *Good Souls, Bad Souls and Assholes* and couldn't put it down. The ups and downs of the birth complications with Eric—her pride and joy—relationship drama, and the rawness of her story had me on the edge of my seat wondering what would happen next. Her passionate words, filled with a mother's love for her bundle of joy, transported me to the very moment as if he were just born yesterday. Listening to her describe miracle after miracle of his will to live and her resilience to survive despite the odds against her was riveting.

At times throughout reading her book, I felt her pain and then suddenly starting cheering her on as an executive coach in her many roles as CEO in a male dominated world. My favorite story is when she said…well, I can't give it away. You have to read the book. It's just that good. Here's a hint, she flipped the script on the men in the boardroom and ended up receiving double her salary. Ballsy…very ballsy. Bravo, Tina.

This is more than a book and more than a random collection of stories; this is a manifesto of a renaissance woman who refused to allow any setback to handicap her destiny. She has the gumption, backbone, intellect, and a velvet chain saw to cut to the heart of the matter of any situation in a nanosecond. If you are lacking in fortitude, faith, and the favor of God, by the time you put this book down, you will have a fire lit within you that will burn out any doubt in yourself or anyone around you.

This is one of the most important books you can ever read. My daughter is fourteen, and I want her to read it. I realize that it may be way over her head, but I believe she will get it. I want every man and woman I know to read this book. It's just like a fine wine—it will only get better every time you reread it.

Tina, I raise my glass to you. This is a masterpiece and maybe one day we can see it on the silver screen. Thank you for giving us the permission to recognize the good souls that help us, call out the bad souls that block us, and use every asshole as a steppingstone to a brilliant tomorrow.

Simon T. Bailey

Simon is CEO of *Simon T. Bailey International*. Dedicated to teaching individuals and organisations how to be brilliant in an average world, Simon is the creator of the *Shift Your Brilliance* system and former Sales Leader of Disney.

# Preface

*To understand the heart and mind of a person, look not at what he has already achieved, but what he aspires to.*

—Kahlil Gibran

**I'VE LIVED A** full and colourful life. Those who know me, know of my life-long love affair with theatre. My life, thus far, has had all the drama of ancient Greek Theatre, with all its comedy and tragedy.

"Tina you haven't lived long enough to have experienced all that!" These words often echo through my mind. They were the words of a dear old soul, Jenny, who was in my Bible study class in 1990. I had shared some of my experiences in the safe space of the group. I wonder what she would say to me now, twenty-six years and several significant experiences later?

Soon after my son Eric's birth in the early eighties, I knew that I had to tell his story. I knew that I had to let people know that God does answer prayer. I had to give God the glory for the many miracles that saved the life of my precious son.

However, life rarely goes according to plan. It has twists and turns. It fills up with duties and struggles and opportunities and people. And, so, I kept postponing writing my book, even though I had had several prompts by the Holy Spirit to move forward with it. Over the years, I often told my family members that I needed to write a book. As the big events in my life unfurled, they would say, "Well, there's another chapter for your book"!

My physician implored me to write a book on my recovery from Myalgic Encephalomyelitis (ME), commonly referred to as Chronic Fatigue Syndrome. He said, "Your story will give others hope, Tina." I did want to share my recovery so that others can recuperate as fully as I did, but then I realised I had no more than a single paragraph to write. The only advice I could give anyone was to eliminate as much stress as possible, go on the Candida diet, and get on your knees and pray, *believing* you will be healed.

Then in 2005, I met Simon T. Bailey in South Africa. "You have a fascinating story and should write a book", he said to me. "There are many people who would benefit from reading your story". He went on, "Record CDs, make videos, get your story out there!" At that stage, many of the stories included in this book hadn't even happened yet, but the story of *My Miracle Child* was remarkable and needed to be told. Simon had also listened carefully as I had shared some of my business and leadership stories, and he encouraged me to also write a book on leadership. Stay tuned…

I've often said truth is stranger than fiction when referring to my life. I've had the title of my book, *Good Souls, Bad Souls and Assholes!* for many years. In 2008, I shared the title with Karen Cook. She was astounded when she heard it and said that one of her friends in Cape Town, a metaphysician, had used those exact same words when he spoke to her about a paper he had written. This alarmed me and I said, "No, Karen! That's my title"! Karen arranged for me to speak with her friend and we had a fascinating conversation. When I told him about my book title, he gave me his blessing and said, "That's fine. Use it. I've never officially put those words into print. Use it".

Late 2010, I decided that I would write a book on the intriguing characters I'd met on my world travels. I had already travelled extensively, but in that particular year, 2010, I'd been away from home for almost eight months and had visited sixteen countries on six continents. I wanted to tell the fascinating stories of the entrepreneurs and incredible philanthropists I met, along with the cultural faux pas I made. When I started to write, I realized that I needed to tell my own story first. Also, I was preparing to leave South Africa to join my son in New York and I wanted to write to 'end that phase' of my life. I wanted to let go of my divorces, my whistle blowing and my heartbreak of Eric relocating to the USA. When I began to write this book, I instinctively felt that the timing was not yet right. Revealing the truth at that stage would have had serious, negative repercussions. So I waited.

Then something happened that made me begin writing in earnest. In 2015, I had a health scare. It was May and I was desperately unhappy. I was two months into a new job, which I hated. The job drained me and, as I became more and more depleted, I got ill. When I miraculously pulled through, I knew that it was time to write the book and share with others that there is always hope, because God is mighty.

Additionally, over my years of coaching others, I realised that sharing stories is very powerful. Stories have the power to heal, encourage, uplift and give hope. I knew that every time I shared one of my stories in a coaching situation, it made a positive difference. I also noticed that just listening to people and then offering ways in which I had coped with similar circumstances in my life enabled them to say, "If she went through this and survived, so can I".

If even one person who reads this book is encouraged to fight through life's challenges and become resilient, then I have lived on purpose. And who knows? Maybe more than just one reader will be given hope.

I trust that both the humour and pathos of my true stories, shared here in short chapters and not in chronological order, will give my future grandchildren a glimpse into who *Yiayia Tina* really was—Photinee Sikiotis, a Greek South African woman who stood up, looked up, reached up, spoke up, and held up!

Dear Readers,

Names, dates, places, and incidents in this book have been changed or omitted for a variety of reasons, including but not limited to the security, safety, and wellbeing of the people, places or agencies involved. Any resemblance to anyone living or dead is purely coincidental. I will leave it up to you the reader to realize what is what, who is who, and where is where.

Thank you for reading my stories.
Tina

# Eric, My Miracle Child

*Here I stand, I can do no otherwise; so help me God!
Amen.*

—Martin Luther

**MY MIRACLE CHILD,** Eric, was born in the early eighties. It was exactly nine o'clock at night. I was only twenty-one years old at the time. My pregnancy had been fairly problematic, in that I was living in Zululand in temperatures of 38-42 degrees Celsius and I was working extremely hard with my husband and his brothers, who were our business partners.

Our business, Basil's Supermarket, was a large general store with a grocery section and a diner. The business was located in a farming community, Pongola, Zululand, a rural area that grew sugar cane. Life there was remote, rustic and very basic. Life there was hard.

I had had a fall when I was just over eight months pregnant, as well as some other discomfort, which led me to go up to the Transvaal to the town of Elangeni, where my parents lived, one week before my baby was due. I was determined not to have my baby in Pongola and, thank God, I didn't.

When I arrived in Elangeni, I had what we called "a show" in those days, or bleeding. I had never had a scan or even a gynecologist. I reckoned that I wasn't the first woman to have a baby and I certainly wasn't going to be the last. And, so, when there was a bit of bleeding, I alerted our general practitioner, Robert Graham, who also happened to be my mother's neighbour, and he told me that I had to go for a scan. The scan only revealed that the placenta had moved, something that wasn't abnormal a week before the due date.

The baby's due date came and went. During the four days that ensued, I suffered a lot of trauma due to a message I had received from my husband Jim that said that one of our creditors had asked for their money, which we couldn't pay, and that he had declared us insolvent. It was a shock. I was especially concerned, because my father had lent us the money for that business. Fortunately, we were able to pay my father back later. The creditor also owned the apartment we lived in above the store. He shut the business down and then notified us that he was about to throw all our personal belongings out onto the street and would lock the apartment.

### LABOUR OF LOVE

During the four days after my due date, I was primarily concerned with getting my belongings off the street in Pongola and back to Elangeni where my parents lived, as I was not going to be returning to Zululand. At that point, I had no home and no business.

On the day Eric was born, I was eating breakfast with my mom when I realized that I was in labour. I still had to get to the bank and to the removals company, who were going to go and collect my furniture, so I didn't say a word. At that stage, the contractions were about twenty minutes apart, so I was able to hide it and quickly showered and got dressed.

My mother accompanied me to town to arrange for my things to be brought to her home, while I went to the bank to withdraw my personal money (if the creditors pursued the bankruptcy, they would take everything we had). For more than ten years, I had saved the pocket money my dad gave me and nobody had a right to my money! At this point, I still didn't know what had gone wrong with our business. My husband arrived at my mother's house while we were in town.

I was able to get through the whole day in labour without anyone being the wiser, but by three o'clock in the afternoon, I couldn't hide the contractions anymore and told my mother. She took me straight to Dr. Graham's consulting rooms. He examined me and said, "Yes, you need to go straight to the nursing home". I replied, "No, I don't have my little suitcase that I packed with me". And, so, my mom took me all the way back to her house where I was able to say goodbye to my bed-ridden grandmother who lived with us and tell her that, when I came back, I would have my baby with me.

When I arrived at Saint Agnes's Nursing Home, the Nursing Sister told me that I still had a very long way to go, and she brought me tea and some biscuits. This cost me dearly because, a couple of hours later when they realized they had to do a Cesarean, they wanted me to wait a full four hours because I had eaten. By that stage, I was upset. I was in heavy labour and, on top of having to endure four more hours of contractions, I would have to have a Cesarean.

Then I overheard the sisters in the hallway talking on the phone to my doctor in Afrikaans. I think they thought that the Greek woman couldn't possibly speak Afrikaans. But I could understand very well. My Afrikaans was excellent and, in fact, I had produced plays in Afrikaans. The nursing sisters were telling the doctor to get to the hospital as fast as possible be-cause my water had broken and there was meconium in the water. I didn't know what that was, but later discovered it was a sure sign of fetal distress. Dr. Graham arrived and confirmed that the Cesarean had to take place and would be performed at nine o'clock. I just wanted it over because I was in a lot of pain. I was also in a lot of pain psychologically because my husband had arrived—he was never supportive, but never less so than on that night—and he had invited a friend along. He and his friend, Neil, stood on the balcony of my room talking and smoking, as I was in labour and about to go into surgery to have my baby.

### COMPLICATIONS

I was wheeled into the operating theatre. When I awoke, I knew that something was wrong. Doctor Robert Graham entered my room. I knew Dr. Graham very well and could tell from his body language that something was wrong. He sat on my bed and said, "Congratulations, you have a son. You have a son and I'm going with him to Johannesburg Hospital", which was the big teaching hospital in the Transvaal province. "The helicopter is taking him to Johannesburg Hospital because he has exomphalos." I did a very quick translation into Greek and it literally means "outside belly button". Dr. Graham explained to me that he wasn't certain what to do, as he had never seen exomphalos before, but that Eric would be in good hands and he would let me know how things were going.

He was very cut-up when he told me. I could see that he was close to tears. I reached for him as he got up, but I couldn't touch him because of my pain. In fact, I couldn't move. I felt as though my legs had been cut off. But I said to him, "Dr. Graham, if it's bad, don't help him".

No matter how often I've told this story, I still go cold when I share it. I didn't know what exomphalos implied. I didn't know if it meant my son would suffer forever. I didn't know if it meant he would be mentally retarded. I didn't know anything. I didn't want the doctors to save him, if he were going to be chronically disabled. I go cold because it really is the wrong thing for a mother to say and I am ashamed. Where there is life, there is hope. I have asked God for forgiveness that I even thought along those lines. God is good and God does perform miracles, and He was about to show me that.

I spent three days in the hospital. I had to stay there to finish an intravenous serum for Rhesus factor. During this time, I'd get reports twice a day about the progress of my baby. They said that he had had major surgery and that it was successful. The minute I finished treatment, I asked to be released so that I could go see my son.

## JUST IN TIME

A dear childhood friend of mine, Theresa, worked at Johannesburg Hospital and came to see me. She told me she had seen Eric, that he was in an incubator, and that the doctors were surprised at how well he was doing after such a major operation. But I couldn't visualize any of it. I didn't understand the explanations given me. Finally, I realized that the situation was new to everyone, which made it difficult for them to convey information to me clearly. I couldn't wait to go and see him.

On the fourth day after Eric's birth, my husband came to take me from the nursing home to the hospital in Johannesburg. Before I left the nursing home, the doctor told me to make sure to use a wheelchair when I arrived in Johannesburg, because the hospital was enormous and I wasn't really fit to be walking those long passages. I didn't ask for the wheelchair, but walked as fast I could to go see my baby. As we were walking down the corridors, my husband had the cheek to say to me, "Please don't cry when you see him. I don't want to be embarrassed." Unbelievable. What an asshole!

What I saw next was a dreadful scene. Unbeknown to me, the doctors were so pleased that Eric was doing well, that they took him out of the incubator, out of intensive care, and moved him to a general ward and into a little cot. They had been too ambitious.

Thank God I got there when I did! As I reached for my baby and touched him, he was ice cold. I screamed (to my husband's disgust). I screamed for a doctor. An Israeli house-man—a houseman is a doctor in training—came running.

"Something's wrong! Something is wrong with my baby"! I said. He told me to step aside and calm down. Then he picked up the baby, called for help, and whisked him away. I had seen Eric literally for two seconds. I hadn't even held him, but had just touched his little arm.

They took Eric away into a small theatre that was on the floor in the pediatric ward. I could hear him screaming and screaming and screaming, and there was nothing I could do! The screaming went on for ages, until they wheeled him out in an incubator.

How it broke my heart to see him like that! Eric had inch-long black hair, half of which had now been shaved off. They had placed an intravenous drip into his head and secured it with white Plaster of Paris. There was also a tube coming out of his stomach, which I later learned was a drain. Apparently, the wound on his stomach, which I hadn't even seen at that point, had become septic. I had reached him at exactly the right moment, by God's grace, and they had been able to give him an intravenous antibiotic. They put him straight back into the incubator.

I asked if I could touch my baby. They allowed me to put gloves on and reach into the incubator to touch him. How glad I was to be able to touch him and pray for him! After only four or five minutes the matron came along and told me that I had to leave, that it was time to go. I prayed to God that there could be a way for me to come back and not leave again, until it was with Eric in my arms. It tore my heart to shreds to leave my baby. As we drove home, I was very distraught, but trusting God...trusting that there was nothing I could do for my son that God couldn't do.

## TOGETHER AT LAST

My family had some close friends who were medical people, and we were very privileged to have a friend, George Louridas, who was a doctor at Johannesburg Hospital. It was he who made it possible for me to stay at the hospital, so that I could be close to Eric.

Yes, we pulled some strings, thank goodness, and I was able to stay at the hospital. However, the policy was that I could be there only if I were breastfeeding. And I couldn't breastfeed. The shock and trauma of the experience, the Caesarean, and the separation from my baby for four days, stopped my milk. But we started a course of tablets to bring on the milk. I started eating and drinking as much healthy milk-producing food and drink as I could. And my father, bless him, bought me stout. "I can't have too much of that", I said forcing a smile.

At the tender age of twenty-one, I had already learned so much. What a joy it was to be so close to my baby! And what an enormous blessing it was to watch him miraculously pull through every hour! Professor James Charles, the physician that performed the operation on Eric the night he was born, came around every morning and evening with the housemen. It galled me to hear them speaking about Eric, as if I weren't even in the room. They said things like, "If he gets to the such-and-such a stage" or "if he overcomes xyz..." It was clear that they did not expect Eric to survive. However, I could see that, day after day, the Professor and his housemen were surprised at Eric's progress.

I kept quiet for four days but, on the fifth day of listening to the chatter, I could not contain myself. On this day, when the Professor and his housemen began their negative talk, I stood up, all five feet of me, and I puffed out my chest, and I said, "Excuse me, Gentlemen, you have forgotten that there is a God". They were all astounded. No one said anything. Finally, they resumed their medical speak, writing on their clipboards, prodding, examining, and ignoring me. Later that day, they sent over some medication for me. When I asked the sister what it was, she replied that it was a tranquilizer. I refused to take it, of course, because I didn't need a tranquilizer. I was stating a fact. These were men talking science and, yes, they had forgotten that there is a God and that God was hearing my prayers.

### MY GREATEST LIFE LESSONS

The days I spent in the hospital with Eric were my greatest life lessons. I learnt so much about the dedication of those nursing sisters and how they endure all sorts of trauma, and how they cope. I also assisted them with some very basic duties during some evenings, because they were so short-staffed. It was an absolute eye-opener to be there. I was the only mother there with her baby, so it was the nursing sisters and me at night. They taught me a lot. They taught me to be very firm when I deal with the baby and not to be hesitant at all, but to clasp him firmly. They taught me how to feed him and how to weigh him. They taught me all sorts of things that I needed to know.

Eric defied science and got stronger with each passing day. On the fourteenth day after his birth, the doctors told me that they'd watch me bathe and handle Eric the following day and, if I were competent enough, I'd be able to take him home. I got very, very excited because, initially, they told me that, if he survived, he would need to be hospitalized for a minimum of six weeks, in addition to needing another surgical procedure. We were only at the end of the second week and so, I was full of praise and thanks for my miracle child.

I asked the sisters to show me how to bathe him, something I hadn't yet done. There were no facilities in that ward for bathing babies. So, the following day, the sisters brought a great big cooking pot to serve as a bathtub for Eric. I bathed him and they were quite happy with the way I handled him.

The sisters told me, "Don't be scared. Just touch him and be firm, so that the baby feels secure and also so that he doesn't slip out of your hands. Show the doctors that you know how to handle him". The doctors arrived. I passed their test. And then they said, "You can go home, but with such major surgery and separation from the mother at birth, we expect brain damage". I was horrified. When I asked to what extent, they replied that they didn't know. I remember asking, "Will he be slow or will he be retarded?" Once again, they said they couldn't tell until he was of an age that they could start doing more reflex tests. They also told me that I had to bring him back every week to be examined as an out-patient and that they suspected at six weeks, the pediatric cardiologist would have to assess whether he could have a heart operation or whether we had to wait until he was older. That was the first time they had mentioned that something was wrong with Eric's heart. I asked for an explanation and they told me that Eric was born with two holes in his heart. You can imagine how shocked I was.

Every hour with my baby alone meant that he could heal. I knew that Eric was incredibly strong and a fighter. For example, even as a newborn, Eric had pulled out all the tubing from his head and stomach. When I arrived at the hospital on the fifth day after his birth, there he was... on his back, ankles and arms tied with bandages and pinned to the underlying mattress in the incubator. They had crucified him! When I asked why on earth they had done that, the sisters explained that he kept pulling out the drip and the drain, and that he was so strong, that they had to restrain his arms and legs. It was traumatic to see his little limbs tied down, but I knew that this was for his own good and that, yes, he would fight tooth and nail to survive.

## ERIC COMES HOME

While bringing Eric home to my parents' house was a joyous occasion, it was also quite a difficult one. Family and friends wanted to visit, but it wasn't safe for Eric. He had come out of a sterile environment and, unfortunately, people carry germs and I didn't want them around my baby. Add to this that I now had no home of my own and all my belongings that had been tossed out into the street were in storage somewhere.

My husband, Eric and I were staying in a little room that used to be my mother's art studio. It really was a very small space for the three of us, but I was happy to be in my parents' home. My father was an incredible support. He got up with me whenever Eric needed something. This was no small feat, because Eric needed something all night long.

Eric was extremely restless and never slept more than two hours at a time, when he'd wake up screaming. His bloodcurdling screams were quite frightening. They continued until he was almost three years old. It was an excruciatingly difficult time. Nobody could pinpoint what was wrong until he was almost three years old, when he had his tonsils and adenoids removed. It was then that he slept through the night for the very first time. The reality was that, up to that point, my child could not breathe very well. Apparently, he had adenoids that were larger than an adult's. Once they were out, he could breathe and he slept soundly.

I doubt that I would have survived that period without the loving support of my family. Several members played a role. My Mom read up everything there was to know about my child and relayed the valuable information to me. She cooked healthy meals for me. She kept well-meaning visitors away so I could rest and Eric wasn't exposed to germs. My maternal grandmother, who lived with us, had had a stroke eight years before Eric was born and was bedridden. During the ongoing challenges and sleepless nights with Eric, I found great comfort in sitting next to her and talking with her. She had lost her speech with the stroke, but we understood one another. How glad I was that she had had the opportunity to meet Eric and to love him. It brought her such joy! She passed away when Eric was about eleven months old.

My paternal grandmother was fit for her age and an incredible human being with an amazing drive and zest for life, and she was a great support to me emotionally. While my husband was anything but supportive, my parents-in-law were phenomenal and assisted me whenever and however they could. My brother-in-law, Roger, was very dependable and he loved Eric dearly.

My sister is five years younger than I am and so she was in the height of her teenage years when Eric was born. Although she adored Eric and could help out when needed, she couldn't be an emotional support in those years. However, in years to come and now, she is a tower of strength to me. She is an absolute darling, and I adore her. I cannot imagine adult life without her. But at the time, she was preoccupied with school, friends, and growing up. As Eric grew, she grew closer to him and called him "little brother" because they are only 16 years apart. And when she started working, she spoiled him with gifts, outings and lots of laughter.

My brother and his wife visited often and my sister-in-law was able to babysit Eric to give me a few hours of sleep. Between her and my mother, I was able to grab a few hours of rest here and there to keep me going.

To this day, when I hear new parents expressing their exasperation that their babies are still waking for a midnight feed, I look back with amazement that I made it through that epically challenging period. Until he was about eighteen months old, Eric had to be near me. On rare occasions, he could part with me for more than a couple of hours to spend time with my mother, my mother-in-law or a friend, but, generally, I needed to be there. I did not take a full day's break until he was eighteen months old.

Eric was a miracle. With every weekly examination, the doctors were more and more impressed, and increasingly positive that he would survive. I knew that he was a chosen child…that he was an extremely special miracle baby. I talked and read to him, and I would not allow anyone to pity him. I instructed anyone who visited him, including my parents, to treat him as an absolutely normal baby. It paid off.

### THE MIRACLE CONTINUES

The doctors actually started to marvel at Eric. By the time he was about six months old, Professor James Charles started to call Eric "the Professor". All the reflex tests showed that he was more advanced than the average baby of that age. This has continued, praise God, throughout Eric's life.

When he was a year old, Professor Charles said that Eric was ready to go see the pediatric cardiologist. I was nervous. They hooked him up to a monitor. The Israeli cardiologist kept exclaiming, "Oh, my God! Oh, my God"! I had no idea why and asked him what was wrong. He replied, "Listen".

"I don't know what I'm listening to", I said.

Then he described how both holes in Eric's heart had closed on their own. Not only could he see it on the monitor, but he could hear it, as well, through his stethoscope. He described the sound that water rushing through a hosepipe makes when you bend that hosepipe and the sound is amplified, because the hollow inside the pipe has been almost closed off with the bending. And that is what he could hear in Eric's heart. Eric does, to this day, have heart and lung murmurs, but he never needed to have the surgery. And the little Israeli (he was little, less than five feet tall) actually called it "a miracle", which was a phenomenal thing to witness.

After that, they decided that Eric needed an operation to remove one of his testes. He had an undescended testis, something that is quite common in little boys, but his was in the stomach cavity and not in the canal where an undescended testis generally resides. I had to sign documentation that, if they found that it was dangerous because of being foreign tissue in the wrong place, they would remove it because it could become cancerous. Well, Eric came out of that surgery with a smiling Doctor Charles, who said, "Not only was it normal, but I was able to bring it right down and put it in its place. We'll monitor it and, in years to come, it should function normally". Another miracle!

When Eric was in grade three, he was selected to go to a gifted school. In his final year of school, he achieved distinctions. With very little effort, he passed first-year University with outstanding results in all his subjects. And then his career began. I'm very humbled, but proud, to say that he is one of the best in the world in his field. He has won multiple awards in the workplace. He has published his work, given trainings, and delivered presentations and speeches globally. Eric is just phenomenal. Bless him.

### PRAISE GOD

Eric has always been my strength and inspiration. He has always been my greatest supporter. I've always told him the absolute truth about everything in every situation. He was with me through both divorces. He was with me through my illness. He was there to support me through my whistleblowing. He was there to edit my work when I was CEO and dealing with the media regularly. He was there when my Dad died and when my Mom died. He still is my go-to person, my trusted advisor, my teacher and my mentor. Eric is a miracle life, a miracle child, who has taught me everything that I know about life. Eric is an old soul. He's gifted... very gifted. Praise God.

# Theatre, Alas!

*Theatre was my first love. I can't take the theatre out of me. And I wouldn't want to. To me, it's home.*

—Jim Parsons

**I FELL IN** love with drama at an early age. I remember acting out my own scripted plays for all my friends and relatives. I also attended drama classes once a week and enjoyed every minute. My speech and drama teacher, Catherine Williams, was a spinster and I admired her and her lifestyle greatly. She didn't conform to society and I liked that.

At high school, I acted in the school plays and, with each new play; my role was bigger and more important. Soon, I was playing main characters. This was an extraordinarily happy time of my life. I thoroughly enjoyed being on stage and felt the theatre was my life and that I'd have a career in drama.

I was devastated that I couldn't study drama at university. I had gone for several auditions and had been accepted. But the prerequisite for drama students was that they had to live on campus because television had just come to South Africa and the drama students would need to do TV studies at night. It was February 1977. I was only seventeen years old and my father wouldn't allow me to live away from home. Witwatersrand University, known the world-over as 'Wits', the best university in South Africa, refused to accept me if I couldn't stay on campus.

I wasn't going to give up, though. I joined Elangeni REPS, a repertory company, and I landed a main role the first time I auditioned! I was thrilled. Now I was acting with adult and accomplished actors. I remember one play in particular. It was a risqué adult farce called *Mate in Three*. The tiny revealing dress, fishnet stockings and stiletto heels I had to wear for the role, had dire consequences. The second my father and fiancé saw my performance, my acting career was over. They refused to allow me to return to the stage. So, I decided that I would teach drama instead and earned two teaching degrees. But play practices, producing plays and being on stage were among the happiest moments of my life.

As I lost sight of my dream of being on stage, another dream emerged. I dreamt of owning a home in Stratford-upon-Avon, the birthplace of William Shakespeare. I had been privileged to visit Stratford several times and yearned to live there permanently to run a Bed and Breakfast. I knew that I could make a good living leading tours to the Royal Shakespeare Theatre and adjacent Swan Theatre. My study of Shakespeare for my Licentiate exams, coupled with my love of his work, equipped me with enough material to lead groups. The Bed and Breakfast could house Eric and me comfortably and also pay the mortgage.

I imagined living happily ever after on the banks of the River Avon.

In 2001 when I could have realized this dream, Eric was not willing to leave South Africa. I could not leave him either. I had lost my parents, my home and even my dogs and so there is no way I would have survived the separation from my beloved son. I accepted that this dream was not to be.

# Accuracy for Safety's Sake

*So much perfection argues rottenness somewhere.*

—Beatrice Potter Webb

**I WASN'T ALWAYS** a stickler for accuracy. That came into play when I married Horace Jones. I worked for him from the time we were married, and so I very quickly realized that if I made any mistakes, even little ones, he would blow them out of proportion and a huge argument would ensue. Given that he was abusive, I would have done, and did do, anything and everything to avoid such conflicts. And, so, I taught myself to be very detail-oriented and accurate to a ridiculous degree. Whether it was the written word or numbers, I was fanatical. Even though I had no financial background other than some accounting classes in school, I knew exactly what was going on in terms of the financials of Jones's business.

How accurate was I? I was so accurate that when the auditors brought the annual financial statements around, I was able to pinpoint inaccuracies immediately. By the second year, the auditor, confessed, "You frighten me Tina. We're qualified accountants and you find the errors that we didn't catch".

In order to survive, I became a perfectionist in every area of life. In fact, my husband required it to a frightening extent. I remember going with him to the movie theatre to see *Sleeping With the Enemy*. That movie described my life to a T! I had to be the perfect wife…not a healthy scenario at all.

After Horace Jones and I divorced, I began to relax. I began to adjust my behavior. For example, I would often leave my bed unmade or crumple a towel so that it wasn't hanging straight, or purposely kick the bathroom floor mat so that it was wrinkled, just to make things look a bit untidy. It was my way of undoing some of my perfectionist habits. I'm happy to report that, although I'm naturally neat and like order, I am no longer a perfectionist.

# Tiny Tina

*It's all in the mind.*

—George Harrison

**MY NIECE ANGELINA** was only six months old when my sister, Selina, and her husband, Alan emigrated to Greece. While Angelina was growing up across the world, we spent a lot of time together on the phone and communicating through letters, postcards and videos. However, it was not until Christmas 2004 that we saw each other again. Angelina didn't remember that we had met previously because she was only an infant when her family moved to Greece. But we knew each other very well remotely and I assumed that our in-person meeting would be quite natural.

However, when my sister and her family came to greet Eric and me at the airport, Angelina, who was now seven years old, was visibly upset and looked at me as if I were a total stranger. I assumed this was because she was extremely shy and, also, because to her, it felt like our 'first' meeting.

Back at the house, Angelina stared at me strangely the whole day. That evening, I went into her room to say goodnight and tuck her into bed. I prayed with her and, after I said, "Amen", Angelina continued the prayer.

"Dear Lord, please help Aunty Tina to grow taller. Amen".

It took all my self-control not to burst out laughing. From my voice, my language, and the stories she had heard about me, this dear child had imagined her Aunty Tina to be "larger than life". Naturally, she was disappointed. She had expected a tall, statuesque aunt, not an aunt who was barely five feet tall.

Angelina remained concerned throughout our visit. On our last night together, I prayed with her at bedtime. After the Amen, Angelina said, "Aunty Tina, when you go home to South Africa, if you go and join a gym, maybe they'll stretch you".

Out of the mouth of babes…size does matter.

# Empath

*Some people are far more cognizant than others but sensitivity has its own cross to bear and ample insight, in many cases, can bring on disquietude.*

—Donna Lynn Hope

**I AM, IN** the true sense of the word, an "empath". This means that I feel what others are feeling and, oftentimes, suffer along with them. As I got older, I began to understand this aspect of my character, inherent from birth.

From a very young age, whenever anyone around me was arguing, I would start to cough. Even then, I hated conflict. I feel it. I suffer for it. My mom adored my dad and used to call him "my beloved husband, my strength, my best friend", and… "my sparring partner". When my parents argued, I suffered physically, even though their arguments were nothing out of the ordinary nor any different from what other couples experience. However, I felt the discord acutely and would begin to cough.

## TRAGEDY

A strong indicator of me being an empath appeared when I was only eleven years old. We were living in Durban, which is on the east coast of South Africa. My father had worked incredibly hard for three years in a business that he owned with partners, called Alpha Ship Chandlers. Ship chandlers are retailers that supply ships with everything they need— from makeup for the captain's wife to heavy machinery, food, or spare parts for the engines—whatever a ship needs as it comes into port for a couple of days or, sometimes, even for just a couple of hours, before it leaves again. And, so, my Dad worked crazy hours.

During those three years, we hardly saw him. My mother used to take us into the city on Friday afternoons to see my Dad at work. There were times he got called to work on Christmas day. Whether it was Easter or our birthdays, my Dad worked. Sometimes, he stayed on the premises for two nights at a time. It was a sacrifice he made to have enough money to give his family the very best. His plan was to build the business and then sell it, so that he could go into something that allowed him to spend more time with us.

His plan worked. He was able to sell Alpha Ship Chandlers at a great profit and immediately invested in another business which, unfortunately, was a dud. Within two weeks of buying the new business, he realized that he had been cheated and that the business was not what it had appeared to be. He lost a huge amount of money. And I felt the stress. My parents did not speak about serious matters in front of my siblings and me, but I could sense the crisis. I could feel their anguish.

## HAIR

My hair started to fall out in chunks. My parents eventually took me to a specialist, who asked my mom, "Has there been any trauma in the family of late"? My mom replied, "Yes, three months ago, my husband lost a lot of money". The specialist then looked at her and said, "This child is stressed. This child has felt the tension." But my mother fobbed it off and didn't think much of it.

And, so, we cut my hair very short and repeated hot olive oil treatments, but all in vain. The doctor said, "All you need to do is to give her high doses of Vitamin B, which is for stress. The rest of her hair will fall out, but her new hair will grow back as the stress lessens".

Well, with the loss of my Dad's hard-earned savings, we relocated back to Elangeni, our home town near Johannesburg. We moved into a house two houses away from my paternal grandmother, who was a great support to the family. I started at a new school and, yes, with the vitamins, a new life and new hope, my joy returned. Before my father lost everything, my hair had been dark brown and straighter. Afterwards, my hair grew back pitch black and curly! To this very day, I'm loathe to cut my hair. When I do cut it to keep it healthy, it is really quite nerve-racking. Every time I cut my hair, I remember my beloved dad asking me,

"Why did you do that?"

I knew that it reminded him of seeing his daughter's hair fall out because of something he had done. He died in 1999 and, yet, all these years later, I still think twice before I cut my hair.

This incident when I was eleven did not visibly affect my thirteen-year-old brother or my six-year-old sister, although they were aware of the situation. The general atmosphere in our home was normal and my parents didn't show their angst. But I felt it. I suffer when people I care about are suffering.

## More of a Curse than a Blessing

I've recently suffered through the trauma of my brother having brain surgery to remove a tumor. I feel deeply for the people whom I love. During this time, I was in daily contact with him, and prayed for and supported him. And I suffered all the while... Praise God he is well and fully recovered.

Perhaps being an empath is genetic? My sister felt our brother's suffering to such an extent that she was hospitalized when the stress she went through manifested physically. Like me, my sister truly cares about her loved ones.

I also feel for people I've just met – strangers - who are in pain. And it's awful. Although it allows me to connect, be present and empathize, it's not healthy. Being an empath is often more of a curse than a blessing because, whilst I try not to take on other people's troubles, I don't always succeed. I have to coach myself often, "This is not your issue. Just be there. Just listen to people. Hugs are much more effective than anything else you can do. Just be there. Don't get sick because other people are ailing".

It is not easy being an empath. I'm always concerned about my fellow human beings and often try to rescue them. This is an extremely limiting characteristic. I do not want to be a rescuer. Most of the coaching I've received and a lot of the self-work I've done is to be able to step away from the rescuer role. I have been increasingly successful in recent years. I will not rescue people. I will empower them, but I'm no longer there to rescue them.

# Detached?

*The bamboo that bends is stronger than the oak that resists.*

—Japanese Proverb

**RECENTLY, A TRUSTED** advisor whom I greatly respect said something weird to me.

"Tina, you have an amazing ability to cope with whatever life throws at you, because you are detached", she said.

I was horrified and disagree with her one-hundred percent. And here is why.

When I speak on resilience, the topic for which I'm best known as a public speaker, I read the body language of my audience and can tell what they're thinking. Their bodies often reveal their skepticism.

"Yeah, right, that's easy for Tina to say. She's calm and in control, and she doesn't have a clue what it is to be in crisis, to be afraid and to suffer".

This always comes up in some form or another during the feedback portion of my talks, when I ask my audience for their honest responses. The elephant in the room always surfaces. Assuming that I have not suffered much in my life, the audience wonders if I'd change my tune about resilience if I had undergone difficulties similar to those such as they've endured.

When I speak on being resilient, I speak with the authority of my direct experience on the frontlines of life's big challenges. For example, my resiliency has helped me rebound from grief of losing loved ones. Divorce (twice). Insolvency. Physical and mental abuse. Unemployment. Separation from my family and inner circle of friends. Chronic illness. The agony of watching family members suffer from gambling, alcohol and drug addictions. Eating disorders. And suicide. The list is long and painful.

How have I survived and, not only survived, but thrived?

Certainly not by detaching!

The one and only reason that I survived and thrived through these severe challenges was my unwavering faith in God.

My professional life has been as challenging as my personal life. For many years, it seemed as if people expected me to break down under the difficulties I was facing and go to pieces. No way! It's only recently that they've taken to criticising what I believe should be championed.

"Tina is a risk taker".

"She moves from one job to another".

"She gave up an executive position for...*that*"?

"Why does she keep shooting herself in the foot"?

I find these comments perplexing because the people who made them already knew the reasons for the job changes, the most common of which was *ethics*. These people have known firsthand that, when my values are compromised, I leave. I leave no matter how prestigious or well-paid the job is.

Unfortunately, one cannot judge the ins and outs of any job until one is entrenched in the job. No amount of research during an interview process can reveal the hidden cancers in an organisation. Often there are systemic problems that require urgent attention. If I cannot fix them or if am required to do wrong to continue in my job, I leave. I leave because I will neither be a part of corruption, nor stay when I cannot add value to the company. My experience runs the full gamut... from corrupt bosses to those who expect me to do repetitive work and, ultimately, to stagnate.

For example, I had a boss whose ego caused her to take her eye off her business and run into cash flow problems, which meant that I had no budget to complete the project she employed me to do. Or the boss whose foul mouth offended every fibre in my body. And then there was the corrupt boss who was protected by her board of directors and, when I blew the whistle on her and the board, my life was threatened.

There was also a job in which I had quickly completed the project that I was hired to deliver and, if I stayed on, I would not be adding value to the company. The worst experience by far, though, was the sabotage and betrayal by the founder and head of an organisation, in which my salary was cut by one-third, with no notice, when she knew that I had just signed a lease on a new home. This betrayal was especially bitter. I had grown the organisation immensely with almost six years of unremitting travel around the world. I had sacrificed my personal life to build the organization, only to have my future, my pension, and all I had worked for, ripped away because, among other things, the founder had remarried and her new husband was eating through the funds allocated for the business.

Did any of this affect me? In the short term, most definitely. In the long-term, not a chance!

"...but you are so strong Tina"!

Oh, how I hate hearing those words! I am not strong. I am not brave. And I am definitely not detached. I feel everything intensely and I hurt deeply. I've been wounded often. I have been burnt. So much so, that I lost my health. For twelve years, I suffered with Chronic Fatigue Syndrome. My personal circumstances of an abusive marriage, coupled with the various workplace stresses, took their toll. But, I'm resilient and, through fervent prayer, I am healthy now. Unfortunately, my body doesn't take well to life's blows and lets me know in no uncertain terms when it is time to be still, reflect and recover. So, while my immune system has been compromised by all the stress and trauma I've experienced, my mind and soul are bulletproof.

Detached? No.

Forgiving? Absolutely.

Accepting? Yes.

Resilient? Yes!

In engineering, "resilience" is the metric used to measure the flexibility of steel when compressed under massive weight. I do have the ability to recover from being compressed, oppressed, repressed and distressed. There is no secret formula, though. Prayer and faith never fail me.

"And we know that all things work together for good to them that love God and are called according to His purpose". (The Holy Bible, Romans 8:28)

I have proven this time and time again.

# Lost In Translation

*Common sense and a sense of humor are the same thing, moving at different speeds. A sense of humor is just common sense, dancing.*

—Clive James

**IN THE LATE** eighties, I bought a bakery in Iliwa and inherited the previous owner's employees. The employees had some bad habits, the worst of which was swearing. They used the F-word prolifically and all day long, no matter how many times I requested them to stop. I'd chastise them and give them warnings, but to no avail. Finally, it dawned on me that they had no idea what the F-word meant. The employees, all local people, were primarily uneducated, and their English was precarious, at best. They used the F-word for anything that didn't work or whenever something broke.

I reached the limit of my patience when, in front of four of my customers, one of my young female employees came to me to tell me that the cake mixer had broken. She said, "Ma'am, the cake mixer is fucked up". The customers saw the funny side of this and roared with laughter. They knew she wasn't intending to curse, but rather, she was using the colloquial language she had heard so many times. But I was very embarrassed. I was also angry. I had told my employees time and time again not to use that word under any circumstances.

Once the customers had gone, I took this young lady aside and told her, "That's the very last time you will use the F-word in this place. Next time you are fired!" I then called a staff meeting and explained to all of them that, if something ceases to work or if they drop something, it is *broken*. It's *broken* and it's not "fucked up".

I went on and on, "A glass, if it drops, is *broken*. If the cake mixer ceases to work, it's *broken*. If the roller for the pastry doesn't roll, it's *broken, broken, brokennnnn*. The next person I hear using the F-word will be given a final warning, if I don't fire him or her first". I had had enough.

A few days later, two of the employees, who were often at odds with each other, got into a heated argument. The coffee shop in the front section of the bakery was filled with customers. My employees' argument could be heard throughout the bakery and, as I walked towards the commotion in the back to tell them to be quiet, one of them shouted at the other, "Just break off"! Instead of chastising them as I had planned to do, I exploded with laughter. The arguing continued to escalate with more and more use of the B-word.

"Break off!"

"Go break yourself"!

# Uncharacteristic
# Word Choice

*Very few big executives want to be surrounded by "yes" men. Their greatest weakness often is the fact that "yes" men build up around the executive a wall of fiction, when what the executive wants most of all is plain facts.*

—Burton Bigelow

**I WAS THE** COO of a Labour Council in Iliwa, South Africa. As much as I hate feeling like a cliché, I was the only woman with ten men on the board. Yes, ten men with giant egos. Five of these men were Union Presidents and five were Employer Body Chairmen.

When I was promoted into this position, I inherited the problem of dealing with an agent in the industry whom everyone knew and disliked because he was bribing officials at the Department of Labour and defrauding shop owners in the Iliwa area. I could neither understand nor accept why nobody had put him behind bars, let alone allowed him to operate.

My perpetual questioning during board meetings fell on deaf ears. The agenda item relating to this unsavoury character was deferred to the following meeting each time. By the sixth meeting, I could not contain myself any longer. When the Chairman told me to stop bringing the matter up because there was nothing that could be done about it, I retorted with, "There has to be something we can do".

One of the Union macho men said, "Tina, what makes you think you can do something, if we can't"?

I am not particularly proud of my answer. In fact, I can honestly say that I was as shocked by my response as everyone else in that boardroom. I stood up (in those days I only wore skirts) and I said, "Gentlemen, if you had the privilege of looking under my skirt, you would see that I have got bigger balls than all of you put together! Either do something about this thief, or I leave". And with that, I picked up my file and my handbag and I walked out.

I sat in the bathroom, trembling and horrified at what I had said. I had always been a lady! I was petrified of the consequences and was convinced that I'd be fired. I needed the salary, as I was still paying the attorneys for my divorce, my mother was ill, and my son was at university.

Suddenly, there was a knock on the bathroom door and the secretary summoned me to the boardroom. I breathed deeply and prepared myself for the worst. I told myself that I had acted like a man and now I must take what I get like a man! I could not look at anyone. The Chairman went on with the agenda as though nothing had happened and when he reached "General", he instructed the secretary to minute: "A full mandate for Mrs. Thomson to approach ABC&D", a firm of highly reputable attorneys, "and to pursue the case". Then he added, "And let's vote to double Mrs. Thomson's salary. We have wanted to reward her passion and commitment for quite a while now"!

I didn't flinch. To this day, I am ashamed of my choice of words.

# Turning 40

*Give sorrow words; the grief that does not speak knits up the o'er wrought heart and bids it break.*

—William Shakespeare

**MY FORTIETH BIRTHDAY,** the twenty-sixth of August 1999, was difficult. For starters, my beloved dad had gone home to be with our Lord in February of that same year, and it was my first birthday where he wasn't there to celebrate with me and to wish me well.

My fortieth also came at the tail end of my marriage to the insanely jealous and controlling Horace Jones. And he knew that he was losing me. He knew that, when I got the job at the Oasis Hotel earlier that year, I was on my way out.

His was a type of controlled panic. Horace Jones's strategy was to hold me hostage by inviting, no, *insisting,* that my mother come to live with us. Because my mother was still grieving my father's passing, I didn't want to upset her by showing that my marriage was crumbling. Even though Horace and I continued to share the bedroom, due to the fact that my mother was in our guest bedroom, we were estranged from one another. Needless to say, I could not count on him for any birthday celebrations.

### Ladies Luncheon

Forty was a big birthday, a milestone, and I wanted to do something to commemorate it. I had overcome enormous challenges and yearned to celebrate my victories with my loved ones. So I decided to host a luncheon for ladies on the Saturday following my birthday. Having a ladies luncheon freed me from needing to include my husband. The luncheon was at Quinn's, a fabulous restaurant filled with photos and memorabilia of Anthony Quinn, my favorite actor of all times. I had arranged with the restaurant for my mother and me to provide all the desserts. We had a grand time planning and making them together.

The ladies luncheon was splendid in every way. I was surrounded by women I loved and who loved me. I was spoiled with beautiful gifts and magnificent cards. (I'm quite sentimental about cards and have kept them all. I still read them, from time to time, and cherish the special effort and wonderful words that people bestow on me). This magnificent celebration was in stark contrast to my dinner with Mr. Jones a few days earlier on my actual birthday.

### Dinner with Mr. Jones

Horace Jones decided that he had better do something for me on my birthday, so he decided to take our family out to dinner. He did not buy a gift for me, which was dramatically different from the extravagant gifts he had showered on me for previous birthdays. I agreed to the dinner with much reluctance, as I knew that he had a knack for being cruelly sarcastic and vicious in public. I was nervous because, whilst I had learnt to handle his malice, my mom and my son were going to be with us.

That evening, Horace Jones was in top form. But after sixteen years of abuse, I had built up my strength and knew it was just a matter of time before I left him. I snapped back at him with some choice words, which shocked my mother.

Throughout dinner, Horace Jones flirted unabashedly with our tall, blond waitress, and then told my son in full voice, "So you see, my boy, that's how it's done! The women go mad when you say certain things and do certain things". His was a sadistic pleasure. Four or five times did he refer to "tall, blond women", and then he took it one step further.

"You see, my boy, these tall, blond women are simply the best and you need to aim for perfection", he said.

I am neither tall nor blond. I stand at five feet tall and my hair is pitch black. The situation was excruciatingly uncomfortable. My mother squirmed each time Jones repeated his words. And then, God bless him, the owner of the restaurant, a handsome man, engaged me warmly, wished me a happy birthday, and told me I'm beautiful and didn't look a day over thirty. Jones heard every word.

Without missing a beat, I said, "Now you see, Mom, that's the type of man I like. Young and with a full head of hair". Horace Jones was old and bald. I knew I had hurt him and it felt good.

Now, it's not in my nature to retaliate, but I was pushed beyond my limit. I regret being nasty, but it happened! Incidentally, I love bald men but Horace hated his baldness and had gone to great lengths to save the little hair he left.

Other than that miserable birthday dinner, my birthday passed without fanfare. Nobody at work knew it was my birthday. I was relatively new in my job at the Oasis Hotel. Apart from a couple of phone calls from family and friends, that was it. Sadness filled the day. What I really wanted was to be wished "happy birthday" by my father.

# The Great Escape

*After having to give up my dream of being an actress and being on stage, followed by giving up my dream of being a happy housewife, I wondered if there had ever been a woman similar to me in the theatre. I searched the library to find a woman who was an actress- short and not a Barbie Doll- from whom I could learn. At five feet tall (my height) and about as un-Barbie Doll as you can get (a lot like me), Ruth Gordon's words were perfect. She said, "Never give up. And never, under any circumstances, face the facts. Courage is very important. Like a muscle, it is strengthened by use. To be somebody you must last." This quote by Ruth Gordon drove me: NEVER face the facts... All my 'miracle' stories come from this premise. In terms of resilience, "To be somebody, you must last," helped me survive serious illness.*

—Tina Thomson

**HORACE JONES WAS** a notoriously abusive, obsessively compulsive and insanely jealous man. He also happened to be my husband. I realized that something was wrong the night before I married him, but I went ahead and married him anyway.

In early 1999, after sixteen years of marriage, I knew that I had to get out. I knew that, if I didn't leave the marriage, I would end up dead.

In our seventeenth year, I separated from him and filed for divorce. Fraught with peril, the divorce took thirteen months. Throughout this time, I feared for my life and the lives of my son and mother.

## Show Me

I learned everything I know about business from my ex-husband. I married Mr. Jones on a Thursday and, come the following Monday, I was working for him. My first big assignment arrived three days after marrying Mr. Jones, when I had to submit a VAT return. In South Africa, VAT, or *Value Added Tax,* is the tax that is added to every purchase and then paid over to the Receiver of Revenue or Tax Department. I am a fast learner and decisive. So I got into my car, hightailed over to the Tax Department, and said to the first person who served me at the VAT counter,

"Show me".

One year later, when our auditor brought the financial statements for signature, he said, "Tina you frighten me", in reference to my penchant for accuracy. Fear of my husband impelled me to be as accurate as I could possibly be to avoid his reaction to any mistakes. And this resulted in me becoming a *'pain in the neck'* when it comes to accuracy. Happily, I have relaxed a bit over the years.

## Looking for Work

Since I worked for my husband, separation meant that I needed to find a new job. With the attitude that I'd take a job, any job, in a safe environment, I picked up a newspaper and applied for ten jobs by telephone. Most calls ended with me leaving a voice message on an answering machine. One of the calls was answered by *Gretchen*, a woman who sounded familiar. She asked the typical interview questions and then invited me to an interview at the Oasis Hotel. As it turned out, Gretchen was Mr. Coeus's daughter. And Mr. Coeus happened to be the owner of the Oasis Hotel and Conference Centre, the largest privately owned conference venue in the province.

When I arrived at the hotel, I realized that I already knew the family. Mr. Coeus's grandchildren went to school with my son, Eric. Mr. Coeus's entire family—his wife, daughters and sons-in-law— worked together in the company. Vlad, Mr. Coeus's' son-in-law, was chairman of a labour organisation and the organisation needed a secretary.

I got the job on a Wednesday and was to start work the following Monday. But I had lied. I had told Gretchen that I was proficient on the computer. Over the next few days, I set out to turn that lie into truth, and took a crash course. I reported for my first day of work with a working knowledge of computers.

### THROWING DOWN THE GAUNTLET

When I started my new job on the first of February 1999, I had thrown down the gauntlet. My husband never, in his wildest dreams, imagined that I would dare to resign my job with him and his son, Mark, let alone take a new job after sixteen years of marriage. The next three weeks were very strained. He made snide remarks and accused me of having an affair with someone at the hotel.

Then, on the twentieth of February, my beloved dad died. We were all in shock. None of the family even knew Dad was ill, a fact he worked hard to conceal. The reality was that he was terminally ill. During the few months that followed, there were many things to accomplish and my husband backed off a bit. My dad's death gave him the time he needed to hatch his masterplan to keep me.

My husband sensed that it was a matter of time before I left him, because exiting his company and taking a new job indicated I had reached the end of my tether. What's more, he knew that I would inherit some money and that would enable me to leave him. Whilst I had everything that money could buy with Mr. Jones, I had no cash at all. He would buy anything I wanted and more, but he would not give me a single rand!

He planned to hold me hostage by 'inviting' my newly widowed mother to live with us. He knew that she loved our beautiful home, and she readily accepted the invitation. Our understanding was that this would be a temporary arrangement until she returned from visiting my siblings in Greece, when she would buy a townhouse close by.

My mom moved in with us in July 1999, and three months later, went off to Greece. And so, for a few short months, things were bearable because Mr. Jones was well-behaved in front of my mom. But then…

## The Attack

Literally four hours after my mom got on the plane to Greece, my husband attacked! It was a Saturday and the horse races were on, so he hurriedly bid my mom farewell, assured her that he would look after Eric and me, service her car, and … and … and …, *ad nauseum*. I took my Mom to the airport. And Horace Jones went off to the races.

When I returned home from the airport, he was there. He had lost all his money and returned home earlier than expected. Mr. Jones was always dangerous when he lost at the races, just as he was always charming and loving when he won. He swore at me as I unlocked the kitchen door, saying that I should have been at home to welcome him and make him lunch. He swore about my mother taking me away from home and he contradicted everything he had promised her only a few hours before.

I snapped. I knew I needed to get out fast.

I called my estate agent and told him that my house was on the market to be sold. Jones thought I was joking. A week later, when the estate agent arrived to put 'show house' signs on my front lawn, Jones went berserk. He physically and verbally attacked me. This was the first time he had done this when my son was home. Eric came to my bedroom to see what was going on and he saved me. My mature, enlightened, gentleman son saved me by wrapping his arms around me and immobilizing me so that I would not continue fighting back. I was enraged and Eric knew I was out of control. Instead of lashing out at his stepfather, he restrained me instead.

"Relax, he is not worth it", he said.

Eric is very strong. He has well developed shoulders and arms from years of exercise and boxing and he just kept holding me tightly. He kept repeating, "Relax, he is not worth it". Jones left the room, embarrassed. I know that it must really upset him when he recalls the incident, because those are the last words he ever heard from Eric, whom he adored. Eric's words must echo in his mind and disturb him greatly.

I gathered my son and left. It was the sixteenth of October 1999.

That night, I had a function at the Oasis Hotel and I was the emcee. By the Grace of God, I managed to do my job with a dislocated jaw and my body aching.

I told the family at the Oasis Hotel that I could not return to my home. Mr. Coeus invited us to stay at the Oasis Hotel, where we'd be safe. When my Mom returned from Greece, he extended the offer to her, as well. I am eternally grateful to

Mr. Coeus and his family for this generous gesture. Because I couldn't pay for our lodging, I worked events for the family. Seeing that I was dedicated and capable, Mr. Coeus enlisted me to do personal work for him and some work for the hotel, too. I was confident that I'd be protected working for him.

# A Brilliant Entrepreneur

*If you're not a risk taker, you should get the hell out of business.*

—Ray Kroc

**ALTHOUGH MR. COEUS** has not had a single day of formal education, he is a brilliant entrepreneur. Self-taught! His family had sent him to South Africa from Europe at an early age, and so he taught himself English and everything else he needed to succeed in business. I learnt so much from him! He was a valued mentor. He was extremely astute, so much so that there was one instance in which Mr. Coeus surmised the bank was charging him too much for his mortgage. He did the calculations, became convinced of the error, and decided to take them on. He dictated a letter to me, which I put into proper English and legal terminology. The bank ended up reimbursing him the equivalent of forty-thousand U.S. dollars: a significant amount of money in those days. Although very few people succeed in challenging a bank, Mr. Coeus did and he won. It wasn't too long afterwards that I began doing all the staff training, PR and labour law for his hotel.

### I Am a Truth Seeker

I've always, always stood for justice. One of Mr. Coeus's sons-in-law was my immediate boss at the Labour Council. He began to have an extra-marital affair. I was in a quandary as to how to handle the situation. What do I do? Do I tell his wife? Do I tell his father-in-law? I decided that it was not my business and that I would tell them only if it began to interfere with the business.

Then, one day, two of the hotel's waiters came to me and said, "We're very upset. We want to talk with you". My boss was keeping his mistress onsite at the Oasis Hotel and he had sent the waiters up to her room with crayfish and champagne. Mr. Coeus had noticed the waiters were not at the function that they were supposed to be working and asked them where they had been when they returned. They would not say, so Mr. Coeus deducted money off their wages.

### Moer-meter

My *moer*-meter was off the charts. In other words, my blood was boiling. (In South Africa, the Afrikaans word, *moer*, is slang for 'to hit or to fight with'. For example, "He is going to *moer* you".)

My boss's affair was not only interfering with business, it was affecting the earnings of loyal staff members! That was it! I certainly was going to tell Mr. Coeus everything. I had to protect the innocent waiters. Disappointingly, Mr. Coeus did not believe me, but defended his son-in-law.

Soon after I spoke to Mr. Coeus about my boss's affair, one of my boss's favoured employees, Alvah, began to bully me. I told my boss that Alvah had contradicted and undermined me in front of the employees, to which he replied that he would not interfere because "Alvah is an invaluable employee". In essence, what he was saying was that I was not a valuable employee.

I had heard rumors about Alvah stealing liquor, so I decided to follow him one night. I discovered that my boss, in an effort to cloak his marital indiscretions, was assigning his responsibility of allocating the alcohol for the various events being held on their vast property to Alvah. This allowed my boss to slip away undetected.

My boss's front followed a pattern. He'd announce, "I'm running an event down in Alpha Hall", for example. Then he'd give Alvah the keys to the liquor store and tell him not to tell anybody, so that he could go off for the night with his mistress. But what he did not know was that Alvah was stealing alcohol and selling it at a *shebeen*, an illicit bar or club where excisable alcoholic beverages were sold without a license.

## THE JIG IS UP

With Alvah bullying me and Mr. Coeus disbelieving me, I figured it was time to leave. I wrote a letter of resignation, made six copies (one for each family member), and signed each one. I left no stone unturned. I included all my gripes, as well as my boss's affair, Alvah's stealing, all the empty promises of commissions and bonuses that had not been fulfilled and the fact that Mr. Coeus did not believe me. I had thought he trusted me and it was unbearable to think that he thought I had lied. I also could not face my boss's wife, who would ask me questions about his behavior that didn't add up for her. For instance, the time that she asked me why I thought her husband was cashing in a life insurance policy was excruciatingly awkward, as I suspected he was using the funds for his mistress. I placed my damning letter on each family member's desk and walked away.

## THE AFTERMATH

My letter stirred up a hornet's nest. Many of the hotel employees loved me and kept me apprised of the situation, even after I had left. They asked me, "What did you write in those letters? The lawyers and accountants are underlining things and holding meetings with the family daily". Naturally I never ever shared the content of my letters with my ex-colleagues.

Once Mr. Coeus's family put out the immediate fires, the family challenged the culprit, and he and his wife left South Africa for Europe. Later, I learned that Mr. Coeus and his family bought out their shares in the company and dissolved their partnership with them.

Three months after leaving, I heard from Mr. Coeus, but I was too embarrassed, cautious and busy to respond. Six months later, he called again. My son and I met Mr. Coeus for lunch. (I took my son with me because I needed moral support). I was warmly received. In fact, it was as if I had never left. It felt good.

Mr. Coeus is a treasured soul, and he continues to teach me about business and life. He is my old Sage. I remain very close to his daughter Leah, who has a heart of gold and whose generosity knows no boundaries. Leah, her husband and their precious family are very dear to me.

# Titans Meet

*Vision without action is merely a dream. Action without vision just passes the time. Vision with action can change the world.*

—Joel Barker

**MADIBA, THE LEGEND,** was about to hand over the presidency. The State was hosting a banquet in Madiba's honour at the Oasis Hotel's vast Alpha Hall that has a capacity for two thousand people. Mr. Coeus had built the Oasis Hotel and Convention Centre, a massive organisation with expansive grounds, thirty conference venues and two wedding chapels, with his own hands. A humble man, Mr. Coeus usually wore shorts and a t-shirt, with a baseball cap on his head. One would never guess that he was the founder and owner of an empire.

On the day of the banquet, The Great Madiba had been driven up a private entrance to get him as close to the hall as possible, because the grounds of the Oasis Hotel are expansive and, as an octogenarian, it would have been be too far for him to walk. His bodyguards sat outside the limousine, whilst he was in the banquet, delivering his speech, and they chatted with the employees of the hotel. When the banquet was over, Madiba came out of the hall and when he was ready to leave, the hotel staff formed a cavalcade for him to pass through. Being the gentleman and remarkable person that he was, Madiba stopped to shake the hand of every staff member and ask them what their role was at the hotel.

Mr. Coeus, who was only a few years junior to Madiba, stood at the very end of the cavalcade near the limousine in his customary shorts and baseball cap. After Madiba had met the chef, the manager, the head waiters and various heads of housekeeping, he reached Mr. Coeus, shook his hand and said, "Hello, what is your name"?

"My name is Coeus", he replied with a big smile.

"And your role at the Oasis Hotel"? asked Madiba.

"I'm the gardener, Madiba", he said. This was not completely untrue. Mr. Coeus loves gardening and planted every single one of the hundreds of trees on the property.

Madiba shook Mr. Coeus's hand one more time and got into the limo. We were all watching the limo drive down the steep driveway, when it abruptly made a U-turn and headed back toward us!

Unbeknown to Mr. Coeus and the staff, Madiba's bodyguards and chauffeur had told him that the old man in the baseball cap and shorts was actually the owner and founder of the Oasis Hotel…the man who had built it from the ground up. Upon hearing this, Madiba insisted they turn around and drive back up the driveway to where Mr. Coeus and the staff were still standing. The state car stopped and Madiba got out. He walked up to Mr. Coeus, hugged him and said, "I like your style", then got back into the limo and off he went.

What a scene…these two legends, such humble men who have accomplished so much, embracing warmly.

# My Dad, My Hero

*I know that I will never find my father in any other man who comes into my life, because it is a void in my life that can only be filled by him.*

—Halle Berry

**I OFTEN WONDER** if I'm single because my dad is my role model of how a man should behave toward a woman. A role model of how a man should protect me. A role model of unconditional love and support. No man has ever come close.

Does such a man exist?

Axios Scott remains my hero. I adored my dad. I respected every word he said...and those he didn't say. I admired his positive attitude, even when things were grim. We laughed a lot.

My dad taught me so much. Not only how to play chess, (he was an outstanding chess player), how to drive, how to shoot clay-pigeons, (he was a national champion), he taught me to always think and act with good intentions. "με το καλό" - "with the good" is the direct translation. He taught me that family is everything.

He showed me that he would die for me. In 1975, my dad took me to Greece for the first time. We toured extensively and then visited the island of Santorini, because that is what I wanted for my sixteenth birthday. We had been on a cruise for a few days and had visited several islands. The day before my birthday, we had taken a small boat from the ship to the edge of the caldera of Santorini. We rode up the caldera's three-hundred-meter steep walls along a chiseled path on the backs of donkeys. After a memorable day in the picturesque, whitewashed village of Fira, we had to descend the caldera on foot. It was far too steep and dangerous for the donkeys to carry anyone and keep their footing.

As we zigzagged our way down the narrow path, the volcano wall looming on one side and a vertical drop to the sea on the other, my dad kept reaching out to me and holding me so that I wouldn't trip and fall. Suddenly three donkeys broke loose from the leather straps that had secured them to a railing at the top of the climb and they started to run downhill! Their metal shoes were worn smooth, and they were slipping on the rock and sliding towards us. My dad pushed me against the rock face and stood in front of me to protect me from getting crushed or knocked over the cliff into the sea.

Of course, there were many times that my dad protected me, but this incident was the first time that I was mature enough to appreciate the extent of his love.

## My Only Regret

I have lived my life without regrets except for one…and it's a significant one. Thinking about this one, phenomenally important missed opportunity, due to Horace Jones's insecurities, is the only time I feel bitter about my marriage to him.

On the fifth of December 1998, my cousin Byron married the lovely Dianna. At the reception, Horace and I were seated away from my mom and dad. In fact, we were at opposite ends of the large ballroom where this grand wedding celebration was underway. I was miserable. Horace had lost his money gambling that day and he was being particularly abusive. I had begged him not to come to the wedding, but he refused to allow me to go alone, so I had to grin and bear it. I had adapted to his jealousy years previous to this and had learnt to either stare at the floor or at the ceiling, but never at any man. I sat trying to smile and "look the part", but I was in inner turmoil. Whilst I was used to Mr. Jones's behavior, this time Mr. Jones was keeping me from listening to my intuition that was screaming, "Get up and go ask Dad to dance".

This very strong message perplexed me because my dad didn't like to dance. What's more, I hadn't danced with my dad since my own wedding to Jim, twenty years prior in 1978. Why was I feeling such intense urgency to go and dance with my dad? It seemed crazy. Did I want a show down with Horace Jones at a family wedding? Did I want drama and a huge uproar when I got home? Was I insane?

I did not go to my dad and ask him to dance because Horace Jones would have been irate had I left him sitting there alone. As bizarre as it may sound, he would have been jealous of my dad. After all, he had been jealous of me spending time with his own sister when she was ill. He had been jealous of me spending time with his granddaughter when I took her shopping, instead of waiting for him at home, just in case he came back from the horse races early. Such is the sick mind of an obsessive compulsive. Mr. Jones wanted to possess me…entirely.

I regret that I didn't defy Horace Jones and ask my dad to dance. This is my one and only regret. Byron and Dianna's wedding was the last social event my dad ever attended. He died two-and-a-half months later. This regret has been a hard lesson, but it taught me to listen to my intuition always. Now I know that my gut feel, or intuition, is a prompt by the Holy Spirit. Nowadays, I pay attention.

## BRAVE AND CONSIDERATE EVEN IN DEATH

My dad was informed that he had cancer of the pancreas, which is very aggressive, but he chose not to tell us. He also chose not to have treatment. I only learnt this fact a year and nine months after he died.

Dad was a gunsmith and gun collector. After my mom died, I advertised his black powder guns for sale in *The Gun Digest*, a magazine that was read by all shooting enthusiasts. Shortly after I placed the advertisement, I received a call from a doctor in Brooklyn who was interested in buying "the collector's guns". Obviously, he wanted to view them first. I arranged to take the firearms to him, along with the permits to transport them.

Before I had even opened my car door, the doctor appeared and asked me if I had the licenses for the firearms. I produced my dad's identity book with all the licenses in it. The minute he saw the photo of my dad, his body language told me that he knew him. Initially, I didn't think much of it because everyone in the shooting world knew my dad. He was a legend. My dad had been awarded Springbok Colours, the highest award in the country, and he had been selected to represent South Africa at the Olympics. (Sadly, he couldn't go to the Olympics because of sanctions against South Africa in those years over apartheid). When the doctor said, "I cannot believe you are Axios Scott's daughter and that I have the honour of owning his firearms", I knew I had the sale!

What I didn't know or expect was that this same doctor was the physician who had diagnosed my father with pancreatic cancer! The doctor related how my dad had simply asked, "How long do I have"? He actually had a lump in his throat and his voice quivered when he told me that my dad had said, "If you tell anyone I'm ill, including my family, I will kill you"! I actually smiled at this and said to the doctor, "And you knew that my dad meant it, didn't you"? The doctor then shared with me that my dad had tears in his eyes when he spoke of his great love for his family.

My dad loved his family so much that he even protected us from the pain of knowing he was dying. He suffered alone. In hindsight, I can pinpoint the day he was diagnosed, the day he surrendered. I can also understand now why he excused himself often from company with trivial excuses that I could not understand at the time. His pain was so severe that he knew he wouldn't be able to hide it, so he needed to be alone. We all thought he was pining for my sister, Selina, her husband Alan and their newborn daughter who had recently emigrated. We thought his weight loss was because he was missing them. Dad adored his youngest child and had not had much time with his only granddaughter. He died seven weeks after being diagnosed. My brave, brave dad.

My mother said that he had been very restless and in the bathroom a lot the night before he died. She kept asking him if he was okay, to which he replied, "Yes". Each time he returned to bed, though, he was weaker. My mom didn't know that he was bleeding internally, something I discovered the following morning when I went into the bathroom and saw blood splattered in the bowl of the toilet. He was so brave that every time my mom said she was going to call the doctor, he firmly said, "No"!

The last time he went to the bathroom, she insisted on calling an ambulance because he was trembling. My father ripped the telephone out of the wall, so she couldn't call. He had a cell phone, but my mom had not learnt the pin number and so she could not use it.

---

My dad was such a proud man that he didn't even allow my mom to nurse him. He most certainly could never have gone to a hospital and had strangers nurse him. He chose to die at home, with dignity, in his own bed.

The shock of my dad's death killed my mother there and then. When I arrived at her home less than an hour after she realized he had passed on and she opened the door, her body was there but her spirit had died with my dad. She could not live without him. One year and nine months of hell later, she took her own life.

# Mom

*"Life throws challenges and every challenge comes with rainbows and lights to conquer it."*

—Amit Ray

**I ARRIVED AT** my parents' home on the morning of my father's death, and was shocked by what I saw when my mother opened the door. Her eyes were utterly devoid of life. It was apparent that Mom had decided life was not worth living without my father.

The irony of this was not lost on me. I've not met any other married woman who is more independent than my mother was…or seemed to be. But the truth of the matter is that my mom was completely dependent on my dad. No one would have ever guessed this to be the case while my dad was still with us.

Mom was feisty. When I was only seven years old, she planned a girl's week away to the Kruger National Park with her friend Gladys. My dad told her very clearly over dinner one night that she should cancel her plans, because she shouldn't go anywhere without her children. She told him that she had the children covered and that our granny was looking forward to having us at her house over the school holidays.

"You are not going", my dad said sternly.

Without responding, Mom continued to clear the table. Several days later, we watched as she packed her bags, the picnic basket and the gas cooker. We watched her as she packed our bags for our visit with Yiayia. My dad always came home for lunch and, when he saw the packed bags, he marched outside, opened the bonnet of Mom's car, and removed something from the engine that immobilised the vehicle. Then he calmly ate lunch and went back to work.

Mom huffed and muttered for a few minutes. Then she walked over to the telephone, dialed and said, "Gladys, there is a change of plans. We are going in your car"! Gladys drove up and we all piled into her car. They dropped us off at Yiayia's house, and then continued on their well-planned trip.

My father thoroughly and unequivocally spoiled my mother. She relied on him entirely and got her own way ninety-nine percent of the time. She derived her strength from him. Mom carried on for another year and nine months after dad died, but it was extremely difficult for all of us. She changed dramatically. Although her body continued to function, her spirit was somewhere else. The fact that she was still alive seemed to cause her great anguish.

My mother became impossible. She acted like a spoiled child. Initially, my siblings and I thought that her behaviour was merely to draw attention to herself. She fell into abject apathy and was listless unless people were entertaining her or she was shopping. Everything she said and did was extremely selfish. Mom, who had come from a very poor family, had enjoyed my father's hard work and generous provision for his family and she spent well. After my dad passed, her spending increased, whilst her activity decreased. Shopping was her drug of choice.

## Moussaka

Mom was a gourmet chef. To this day, I've not eaten any food more delicious than my mother's, including meals prepared by top chefs throughout the world. An artist in every sense of the word, mom had an uncanny knack for combining ingredients that no one else would dream of combining. She had a voracious appetite for culinary books, and possessed an unquenchable thirst for knowledge on a wide variety of topics. Yes, Mom liked to read. Yvonne, my dearest friend, gave the eulogy at her funeral and said, "Juno gave an entirely new meaning to the expression, 'Well read'".

I was at my wits end as to how to engage Mom in life again. Wanting to encourage her and let her know that we needed and wanted her, I decided to buy all the ingredients for moussaka, which was one of her specialties. Knowing that my mom adored her grandson, I tried to entice her to make moussaka for Eric. I figured that, if I asked her to cook for him, she couldn't refuse and would cheer up. And so I asked her and handed her the ingredients.

"I don't know how to make moussaka", she replied.

And that was that.

My beloved Mom…such a brilliant, creative soul! A prolific artist, she used to paint at night when she couldn't sleep. It was not uncommon for her to produce two or three works of art in one day, in addition to her knitting, sewing and crocheting. How could it be that she couldn't or wouldn't do anything?

## From Bad to Worse

My mom became increasingly demanding. She abused the kindness of our friends and family and refused to stay in her own lovely home. Although she had ample income, she often said she didn't have any money and expected others to pay for her whims. No one realised that these were symptoms of depression. I was exhausted and fed up, and it seemed as if she were simply being selfish. She was sucking the life out of everyone and, especially, *me*.

Her shopping increased. Often, when I arrived home at 8:30 p.m. from my second job, she'd show up and ask, "What's for dinner"? Or, she'd crawl into my single bed and refuse to leave. I needed to rest as I had to leave for my first job at five in the morning and it was exhausting to get her out of my bed and send her home to her townhouse in the same complex, just a few doors away.

Exhausted, I would cook dinner for Eric and Mom. She'd criticise the food and tell us how miserable she was, ending the conversation with, "Life is not worth living". I begged her several times not to speak that way in front of Eric. I cherished time with my family and breaking bread together is sacred for me. I could not bear to hear my mother talk this way.

Three weeks before my divorce hearing, she asked me to take her for a drive late at night, knowing I had work the next day. She then asked me to give her a thousand rand spending money. This was the final straw. I was working myself to the bone and in the midst of an extremely expensive divorce.

"Mom, you need to stop, right now", I begged. "Actually, I don't want to see you again until my divorce is final, because you're stressing me out and I cannot bear it any longer".

I adored my mother. Before my dad died, she was my best friend. But, although I'm resilient, I had reached my breaking point. So, while my sanity and equilibrium mandated that she leave, my heart broke.

Friends and family were shocked at what I'd done, but I was in survival mode and needed to be strong for my son. Eric was still mourning the loss of his grandfather. My father had spent a lot of time with Eric. He was Eric's role model.

When Eric turned seven, my dad, a master gunsmith and expert shooter, began to take him to the shooting ranges on Saturdays for "man time". When Eric was eleven, his grandfather invited him to share a beer with him and his shooting cronies. My dad's sudden passing left Eric reeling. Add to the mayhem that Eric had just started his first real job and that my life was in danger on a daily basis during my separation from Horace Jones and our pending divorce. Things were stressful. Although my firm stand with my mother appeared harsh, people close to us understood why I had to set my boundaries.

I did not cut my mom off altogether. When my mom wasn't away visiting friends and relatives, I insisted that Eric visit her regularly. I also sent my beloved housekeeper, Mar, over to my mom's to take her meals I had prepared, clean her house and do her laundry. Between Eric and Mar, I received frequent updates about my mom's well-being.

Oh how I missed the mom I knew before my dad's passing…my brilliant, interesting and precious mom. I mourned her wicked sense of humour. We had had such magical times together… shopping, enjoying tea at beautiful hotels, visiting nurseries to buy plants, gardening together, baking together, and just enjoying one another's company. Even the distance between Elangeni and Iliwa, a full hour's drive, didn't stop us from meeting every Saturday morning to spend the day together. We went on holidays together. She spent a lot of time with Eric and me. And she absolutely adored us. But now, when I needed her more than ever before, I had to keep my distance to keep my sanity. I had to be clear-minded and strong to cope with the divorce case.

## MAR

Martha, whom I affectionately call "Mar", was my housekeeper for nearly sixteen years. When I separated from Horace

Jones, Mar wanted to leave with me, but I couldn't afford to pay her.

Horace Jones and I had resided in my house, the down payment for which came from the money I made when I sold my bakery, The Delicious Oven. I had worked for him throughout our marriage, but received very little, if any remuneration, so even though Horace Jones paid the monthly mortgage, I still came up on the short end of the stick. The house was incontestably mine. When I separated from Horace Jones, he refused to move out of the house, so I had to have him evicted. Mar stayed on for six weeks afterward until the house sold.

When the house sold, Mar left. I was able to find her part-time work three days a week and she worked for me the other two days. It was she who insisted on two days, even though I could only afford to pay her for one day each week.

## THAT FATEFUL MORNING

On that dreadful morning in November 2000, I left home early for work to prepare for an important meeting later that day. When I arrived at my office, there was a message on my answering machine from Mar: "Madam, please call me". The phone rang, just as I finished listening to the message. It was Mar again. She was agitated and insisted, "Madam, you need to come home. The Old Lady is sleeping on the dining room table".

Knowing Mar as well as I did, I was alarmed by the urgency in her voice. I was also angry with my mom. "I've had it! What is Mom up to now? I'm going to go see for myself"! I fumed. I had ample time to drive home and back to work before my meeting.

When I arrived, I parked my car and yelled, "What's going on Mar?"

"I don't know, Madam. I banged on the door and made a lot of noise, but the Old Lady didn't wake up". Mar told me that, when she arrived at my mother's, she had rung the bell, but no one answered. So she went around the back to the garden and looked through the sliding glass door. She saw my mother at the dining room table, asleep, with her head resting upon her arms.

I marched over to my mother's townhouse.

Two weeks prior, my sister Selina had asked her mother-in-law, Vivian, to take Mom to see a psychologist, because she felt that her behavior was indicative of depression. The psychologist had given my mom anti-depressants. Eric and Mar both reported that my mother's emotional state was rapidly improving, day by day. Good news! I had no reason to believe otherwise.

I couldn't, in my wildest dreams, picture what Mar was describing and chalked it up to yet another one of my mother's attention-seeking antics. In the past week alone, I had heard from the complex manager that Mom had put a lit cigarette in a petrol lawnmower. It had also been noted that she left her garage door wide open all day every day. Given that the garage led directly into her home and the crime rate was extremely high in South Africa, this was an extraordinarily foolish thing to do. In hindsight, I realised that both instances were attempts to end her life.

I had the keys to my mom's home and unlocked the security gate. I tried to unlock the front door, but she had bolted it from the inside, so I, too, walked around the side of the house and into the garden to look through the sliding glass door. There was my mother, just as Mar had described, with her head resting on her arms on the dining room table. I banged on the glass and shouted, "What are you doing now? Wake up"! But there was no movement. I still wasn't too alarmed, because my mother, an insomniac, had taken sleeping pills for decades and it was not unusual for her to fall asleep during the day.

I unlocked the sliding door and opened it. As I walked over to my mom, I chastised her for interrupting my day. I said, "Wake up"! and touched her shoulder. She was as cold and hard as marble.

## THE MAYHEM

The shock and horror of the scene still gives me chills now, so many years later, as I relate the story. I had no idea how she'd 'gone to sleep' until I noticed that she was "sleeping" on a piece of paper. Her arms covered most of it, but I could read the beginning at the very top:

> "To My Beloved Children and Beautiful Grandchildren—I'm very sorry for what I'm doing. I can't carry on anymore. Please forgive me".

Time stood still. I saw the beautiful flowers that Eric had given her two days earlier carefully arranged on the table in front of her. She wouldn't let him in that night. He was quite distraught when he came home and said, "Mom, I had to pass Yiayia the flowers through the bars of the security gate. She told me that she was feeling ill and that I should visit another time". I'm so proud of my son! I had taught him early on that flowers should be given to people when they're alive, not brought to funerals. And Eric had given her her very last bouquet.

Along with the flowers, my mom had arranged photographs of all her children and grandchildren in a semi-circle around her. Her Bible was open next to her, too, along with my dad's and her favorite love story, Captain Corelli's Mandolin which she had opened to the passage in which Dr. Iannis is advising his daughter, Pelagia...one of the wisest passages on love in the book. I read the passage weeks later:

> "And another thing. Love is a temporary madness, it erupts like volcanoes and then subsides. And when it subsides you have to make a decision. You have to work out whether your roots have so entwined together that it is inconceivable that you should ever part. Because this is what love is. Love is not breathlessness, it is not excitement, it is not promulgation of promises of eternal passion, it is not the desire to mate every second minute of the day, it is not lying awake at night imagining he is kissing every cranny of your body. No, don't blush, I am telling you some truths. That is just being 'in love', which any fool can do. Love itself is what is left over when being in love has burned away, and this is both an art and a fortunate accident. Your mother and I had it, we had roots that grew towards each other underground, and when all the pretty blossom had fallen from our branches we found that we were one tree and not two. ...."

My mother died of a broken heart.

Her roots, entwined with my dad's had died.

My mother, the artist, had drifted to peace amongst her children and her grandchildren.

In shock, I panicked and called the emergency number. Hysterical, I phoned my cousin, Grace. Then I phoned a dear friend, Gladys. Gladys actually hung up on me the first time, because she had no idea who was calling her in such a state. The fire brigade arrived with the paramedics. Very quickly, they told me that my mom had been gone for at least three hours and there was nothing they could do to revive her. They saw the note. Following protocol for suicides, they asked me to wait outside while they examined the room. About five minutes later, they came outside with the trash can from my mother's bedroom. It held all the empty sleeves of the anti-depressants the psychologist had prescribed, which she had swallowed.

Mar and I sat on the grass holding each other and crying. One of the firefighters, Andre, knew my mother – he was her neighbor - and he was visibly upset. He had befriended my mom and she, in turn, had shared the meals I made for her with his family. My mother was an extremely generous soul, not only with her time and spirit, but also in sharing her material things. The minute Andre ascertained the situation, he hugged me.

I cried, "Phone Eric! Phone Eric! Tell him to come now"! Andre took Eric's number and called him. I asked him to phone my lifelong friend, Theresa, too. By that time, my cousin Grace had alerted a few friends and, within about thirty minutes, my people descended—Theresa and her sister, Mel and their mom, my beloved Thea Mary. These three women were my anchors, my rocks, devout Christians, who immediately began praying over me.

My cousin, Grace, arrived and spoke to the police. And then Eric appeared. Oh, how my heart broke for him! I gathered myself and told myself to be strong for my child. I announced that Eric and I were going home. Thea Mary, who had grown up with my mom and whose family was interwoven with mine, went home with us.

### A BLUR

The news of my mother's death spread like wildfire and, in true Greek tradition, throngs of people descended upon us to sympathise. A couple of people asked me if there was anything I wanted or needed.

"Yes", I said, "I want the minister from the church to come and pray for my mom".

Andre the firefighter was a Christian, too, and I asked him to pray for my mom. I was really worried what would happen to her for having committed suicide, so I needed all the prayers I could get. However innocent and naïve that sounds now, it was my primary concern at the time. A friend phoned the minister at the Methodist church I attended, and asked him to come. The Greek priest from Elangeni was also summoned.

The minister was very comforting. I plied him with questions about what happens to people who commit suicide. His gentle response was that, for someone like my mother, who had done so much good for so many people, heaven was ensured. He then explained how one of his close minister friends had taken his own life because of all the stress he felt from people's confessions. Because confessions are held in strictest confidence and cannot be shared with anyone, the minister had no one with whom to share his burdens and burnt out from the overload.

"We serve a God who forgives, a God who loves. I firmly believe that your mother is in heaven", he said. That's all I needed to hear.

I didn't question further.

As I greeted people, I continued to pray, "Dear Lord, show me. Dear Lord, comfort me. Give me Your peace which surpasses all human understanding. Give me a sign. Let me know that my mom is with my dad". This prayer stayed with me as I tried to comfort my son, who sat alone in his bedroom, unable to emerge and face the large gathering in our small townhouse.

My beloved friend, Athena, arrived. She walked up to me, gave me a big hug and said, "You're the best daughter any mother could have". Incredibly comforting! Eric's close friends, George and James, arrived and kept him company. And I kept praying, "Dear Lord, send me a sign. I need to know that my mom is in heaven".

## Racing Against the Clock

Long before that day in November burnt into my memory as one of the most tragic days of my life, I had already planned to take the following 2 days of November off from work to attend to my divorce. My day in court had been set far in advance and the day prior was to be spent meeting with my attorney.

With my mother's death swirling about me, I suddenly realised that I had to settle with Horace Jones immediately. If he found out that my mother had died, the divorce would take many more months, a few more court appearances, and thousands of rands in legal fees. Horace Jones had already testified in court that he was "a destitute pensioner" and could not pay any legal fees or anything toward a settlement for me. Not true. Horace Jones was a wealthy man, but he had put all of his considerable assets under his son's name. He had pleaded poverty and the courts believed him. He also said that I had inherited a lot of money when my father died.

The reality was that my dad had established a usufruct will, which meant that, although everything belonged to me and my two siblings, we could not access any of the assets whilst my mother was alive, as she was entitled to draw all the income from the properties and other assets. Only on her passing would the assets become the property of her children. When the lawyers looked into it, they could see it was a usufruct will and knew that Horace Jones could not claim against the estate. However, now things had changed dramatically. If Jones found out that my mother had passed away, we would have to reopen the whole case again and thereby extend the severely painful, expensive and bitter legal battle.

As I was entertaining these thoughts, my attorney phoned for a third time. I ignored his first two calls, but realised with this third call that there might be something wrong. He had sent some faxes to my office and, because I hadn't responded, he phoned. I explained to him what had happened. After hearing of my mother's passing, he insisted I postpone the court date. I emphatically told him, "No, absolutely not. This has cost a fortune. I will manage to get through this".

"You're probably still in shock", he said, "And yours is a contested divorce. You'll have to stand up in court. Horace Jones will be there with his lawyers. You'll need to be one-hundred-percent focused and engaged".

Then he explained to me that there were certain things that Horace Jones wanted from me. I never wavered, but repeatedly told him, "Just settle. Settle. Give him anything he wants".

He said, "Mrs. Thomson, I'm going to phone you tomorrow. You're not making much sense". And I left it at that.

The difficult day which followed my mom's passing was a repeat of the day before, with many visitors and well-meaning friends. I hadn't slept at all, as I had been on the phone late at night with my siblings, both of whom were living in Greece at the time. My sister made plans to travel to be with me straightway. My brother couldn't leave because he was in the process of emigrating from Greece to Brazil, and his eleven-year-old son, Axios, was very ill. Shortly thereafter, Axios was diagnosed with Crohn's Disease. Besides this, my brother and his family had seen my mother a few months prior in Greece. No one had known that their time together was one step in her plan to wrap things up before she took her own life.

## Rainbows

The day after my mom's passing, with my home still overflowing with people, I had to step out into my little garden frequently to talk to the attorneys. In between calls negotiating for a settlement, I received a call from a friend of mine who had visited me the previous day. She said, "Tina, step into your garden. Look up into the sky". And there it was! There was my sign from God. Two brilliant rainbows brighter and more resplendent than any I had ever seen. This was the sign I needed that my mom was in heaven with my dad. I visualise these glorious rainbows every time I have a moment of despair. They always uplift me. I remain profoundly grateful to God for His beautiful, beautiful sign.

### BIG SHOES TO FILL

My family and friends were very concerned that I might feel guilty for having laid down the law with my mom. Not for one second! Both God and I know that I had done absolutely everything I could, and more, to please my mother after my father had passed away. My mother had demanded that I step into my father's shoes and I complied. I took over everything for her. I even drove her around late at night, whenever she didn't feel like going home.

"Please take me for a drive to The Ridge, so I can see the pretty gardens", she'd say.

"Please take me for a drive so we can get some dessert".

She often requested that we go out to dinner. Ad infinitum. Her demands never stopped. I did everything I could to please her and ended up incurring significant debt.

I also took her to every doctor and specialist I could find to see what was wrong with her. I could not understand what had happened to my mother. One of the neurosurgeons that examined her at the local Hospital conducted a broad array of tests, after which he told me, "There's nothing wrong with her. She's way above average".

I retorted with, "Doctor, even if she dropped to half of what she was previously, she'd be above average. My mother is a genius".

What followed was quite funny. Not so at the time though. She confided in the doctor that she knew there was nothing wrong with her, but that I was going through a horrific divorce and was heartbroken over losing my dad. The doctor actually looked at me and asked, "Shall I refer you to someone you could speak to"? My brilliant mom had turned everything back on me.

### My Mother's Beautiful Hand

I didn't get to read my mom's farewell letter in its entirety until much later, as it had been confiscated as evidence of suicide by the authorities. Eventually, I was able to retrieve Mom's letter from the bowels of bureaucracy, which was a miracle in itself. Even in her suicide note, my mom's handwriting was beautiful. As it neared the end, though, the script became illegible:

> Sorry, Tina. I did not mean to make things so hard for you. I do love you very much, as I love you all, but I cannot face the future alone. God forgive me.

This was followed by details of her safety deposit box number and some illegible scribbles.

Bizarrely, Mom's suicide letter comforts me. It was my mom's grand finale, the pièce de résistance of a lucid and well-planned departure. Mom mastered everything she attempted. As I reflect on this experience, I begin to see that my mother—a stunningly beautiful woman physically, a generous spirit, a genius, and a gifted artist—was not meant to deteriorate into old age. She was a spry sixty-nine years of age when she ended her life.

At her funeral, my sister Selina and I asked people to remember her as she was, rather than what she became after my dad died. No, that person was not Juno Scott. That person was not our beloved mother. She was a woman in shock who had lost her husband without warning and who desperately missed the one man whom she had adored for most of her life.

## HERMES OF PRAXITELES

My mom always thought of my father as her Greek god. When my father passed on, she wrote several obituaries for the local and national newspapers and, in one of them, referred to Dad as her "Hermes of Praxiteles". The famous statue of Hermes of Praxiteles and my father are one and the same (even though my dad had won a competition in Greece for most closely resembling the statue, the Charioteer of Delphi). My father looked exactly like Hermes of Praxiteles and my mother knew it.

And so rests this great Greek love story…this heart-wrenching tragedy of a woman filled with fire, zest, and love for life, who ended her life to be with her lover. As spirited as my mother was…as independent as she appeared to be…she derived her strength from my dad.

# Back To Negotiating

*The best move you can make in negotiation is to think of an incentive the other person hasn't even thought of, and then meet it*

—Eli Broad

**DURING ONE OF** the calls from the attorney handling my divorce, I was told that Horace Jones wanted everything I had taken from our home returned to him. I had not taken a single thing that did not belong to me. The only things I had taken were articles that had been given to me by my family and friends as gifts and the items I had brought with me when I married the man. Horace Jones had also always given me extravagant gifts... birthday gifts... Christmas gifts... reconciliation or 'guilt' gifts. Although I hadn't taken a single one of Horace Jones's belongings with me when I left, he continued to make requests and, every time, I told my attorney to give him whatever he wanted. There was only one thing that Horace Jones wanted that I refused to give him.

## THE PINK LAMP

When the attorney asked for the various material things on the list and got to the pink lamp, I said no. He was perplexed and said, "Mrs. Thomson, you've given away some very expensive and significant things. May I ask why you want to hold onto the pink lamp"?

"It's non-negotiable", I replied. "Let's move on".

He said, "No, I need to go back to the pink lamp, because it's on the list".

"The pink lamp is non-negotiable", I shouted.

At that point, I needed to say goodbye to the attorney and step inside, because the priest had come again to my home and we needed to make arrangements for my mom's funeral. Very shortly thereafter, the phone rang again and it was the attorney.

"What now"? I asked.

"We've had a note back from Horace Jones's attorney and it states that Jones insists he wants the pink lamp and that it will be a deal breaker if he doesn't get it".

Finally, I explained why Horace Jones couldn't have the pink lamp. I had given it away to Mr. Coeus and his family, the owners of the Oasis Hotel, as a thank you gift for all that they had done for me and there was no way I was going to ask for it back.

The attorney tried to explain to me that Mr. Coeus would understand the circumstances and that we can't settle until we get that pink lamp, and we were almost there, and that he was sure Mr. Coeus would give me the pink lamp back, if I asked. And then he reminded me that I was the one pushing for a settlement. All of a sudden, I got the giggles, because I saw things from my attorney's perspective. He was imagining the item in question to be an ordinary pink lamp with a tiny pink shade, something one would buy for a little girl's bedroom. The more I thought of what he must be thinking, the more I giggled. Obviously it was a nervous, almost hysterical giggle. He was polite and professional enough not to comment but I knew he thought I had lost my marbles; holding onto a pink lamp when I had given away very valuable items and in the process risking no settlement.

The truth of the matter, however, was that the pink lamp is Capo Di Monte porcelain with gold leaf paint. It is most magnificent, about two-and-a-half feet long and boasts a gorgeous woman on a horse and carriage. The base is topped by a silk lampshade, adorned with hand-painted orchids and trimmed with gold and crystal beads. Simply put, the pink lamp was exquisite. It's certainly not something that one would find in an average home. Never again would I be a materialist. And never again would I have a home that was like a museum. I had happily given it away to the owners of the Oasis Hotel, who still have it on display in their formal dining room. The notorious pink lamp was my thirtieth birthday present from Horace Jones and it was mine to give away. I'm sure Jones remembered its value as an original, certified collector's item and wanted it back so that he could sell it.

I instructed my attorney to offer Horace Jones twenty-thousand rand instead of the pink lamp, sure that he would settle because he was a gambler to whom cash was an irresistible temptation. At that point, I hadn't a clue where the twenty-thousand rand would come from, but it seemed a small price to pay for my freedom. Besides, I was already in a lot of debt for legal fees and decided that twenty-thousand rand wouldn't make that much difference. The settlement documentation went through to Horace Jones's lawyers. It was now close of business, with the court date on the morrow.

# "A Real Woman With Testicular Fortitude"

*Power is like being a lady... if you have to tell people you are, you aren't.*

—Margaret Thatcher

**MANY PEOPLE REFER** to me as "very brave". This boggles me. I am not brave. I simply have a clear sense of right and wrong and, when something is wrong, I speak up and act. I know I don't need to be afraid, because God will give me the strength and clarity I need in any given situation. I really don't have many fears, other than the fear of mediocrity.

I was once mortified when I was introduced as a "real woman with testicular fortitude". It seemed a backhanded compliment. When I had a private moment with the head of sponsorship at a big bank who introduced me in that way, I asked, "What was that about"?

He replied, "You are so feminine, but so powerful. You are scared of nothing. You have all of us sitting up at attention. And you get things done without changing your tone of voice, without pounding on the table, and we're just not used to women in powerful positions being as feminine and soft as you are".

From that time on, I made a point of being even more feminine. I softened all my business suits with floral blouses. I let my hair loose and added big earrings to make a point... women can be assertive without being aggressive.

# Quick Change

*My mission in life is not merely to survive, but to thrive; and to do so with some passion, some compassion, some humor, and some style.*

—Maya Angelou

**MY BUSINESS, THE** Sophia Drama Academy, was still in a start-up phase, so I held onto my job at the Labour Council. One of the prerequisites of owning the teaching franchise was that I had to dress dramatically, as if I were on the stage in a full theatre production—a lot of makeup, big earrings, and all sorts of larger-than-life colorful gear that the children, my students, would find interesting. My work attire at the Academy was the diametric opposite of the extremely conservative business attire at the Labour Council that comprised minimal makeup and very little jewelry.

Being both entrepreneur and employee made for a very hectic work schedule. Entrepreneurship is in my blood and I was driven to succeed. From seven in the morning until two in the afternoon, I worked at the Labour Council. From two-thirty in the afternoon until seven thirty in the evening, I taught drama.

Upon finishing my day with the Labour Council, I would practically run to my car in the parking garage. I had the dramatic change down to a science, as I had only five minutes to change from my business suit to my flamboyant drama teacher outfit. I'd open the trunk of the car, quickly change (taking great care not to expose myself), do my makeup, let my hair down and put on bright lipstick, bangles and enormous earrings. Then I'd drive off to one of my studios to teach.

One day, as I was morphing from Labour Council worker to eccentric drama teacher, I felt uneasy, as though someone might be watching me. I looked around, but did not see anyone. I continued my transformation, but sensed eyes on me. Then I heard stifled laughter coming from the car parked next to mine. I looked over and, to my horror; there were two men in the car who had transfixed on my metamorphosis. I can only imagine that they thought I was changing myself into a lady of the night. I was embarrassed. I never said a word. I got into my car and sped off, giggling.

# I Should Have Listened

*To profit from good advice requires more wisdom than to give it.*

—John Churton Collins

**MY SOPHIA DRAMA** Academy was still in its infancy and I needed to earn more money. I had blown the whistle on the Chairman of the Labour Council and resigned. When my values are compromised in any organisation, I leave. And, so, I needed another job, to supplement my income whilst I built my business.

## BEAUTIFUL VOICE

I picked up *The Record,* the local Iliwa newspaper, and faxed my resume to five or six companies that advertised half-day jobs. I taught drama every afternoon and evening, but my mornings were free. One of the companies to which I applied responded almost immediately. The beautiful voice on the end of the phone said, "Your name is Photinee. You are Greek. What is your maiden name"?

"Scott", I replied. The beautiful voice chuckled.

"Tina, I know exactly who you are"!

The beautiful voice was Paul Botes, a man six years my senior, whom I had always considered to be quite handsome. I knew his sister as I had done Greek dancing with her for years.

After interviewing me, Paul said, "You're more than qualified to do the job, but if you were my wife, I wouldn't want you to take this job". I was horrified!

"But I'm *not* your wife and I want the job"! I said. "And I need the job"!

Several times over the next few days, Paul contacted me and tried to discourage me. He said I should withdraw my application. I would have none of it. Eventually, he gave me the job. But I should have listened to him.

### CLICK-CLICK

Paul's worst fears came true. The company was in an industrial area, which was riddled with crime. On the last day of my first month with the company, I had gone to work very early in the morning to draw the end-of-the-month figures off of all the machines and to reconcile them. The job was basic admin work, as I hadn't wanted anything more demanding because I needed my energy for teaching in the afternoons. And my teaching provided more than enough stimulation for my mind.

When I arrived at work, my boss, Charles, was there. We were both completely absorbed in our work. My head was down and my hands were on my keyboard as I pulled the needed passwords from my diary. (This was my first reconciliation, so I hadn't learnt the passwords yet). Charles was at another computer drawing figures he need for his report. And then I heard a sound that I knew very well…the click-click of a gun being loaded. I looked up straight into the eyes of a relatively young man and could see that he was as terrified as I was. I said a prayer for protection and kept telling myself, "You have to stay calm, because he is frightened, and a frightened man with a gun is dangerous". Then he told me to turn around and I could see that there were two others, also armed, and they had my boss at gunpoint.

## SAFE

The three men were desperate. They were scared and shaking. And that made the situation all the more perilous. I was praying that Charles would stay calm, because it was apparent that he was terrified and uncooperative, which added to the danger we were in. By this stage, one of the men who had been holding Charles at gunpoint had come around the counter behind which I was standing, jammed his revolver into the small of my back, and demanded that I open the safe. Immediately, I realized that this must be an inside job, because I was new to the company and very few people knew that I had the combination to the safe. Then he pushed me toward the safe.

I was beside myself because I had never successfully opened the safe on the first try. I thought, "If I don't get it right the first time, they're going to hurt me. They will think that I'm playing the fool". I had written the combination down in my diary and, when I picked the diary up, the movement alarmed them. They thought that I was reaching to press a panic button. The gun in my back thrust forward forcefully. I had heard many stories of robbers firing their guns in a panic and I was very afraid.

"I'm very new to the company", I quickly explained, "and I have to have my diary because the combination for the safe is written in it and I don't know it by heart yet". They agreed to allow me to me to pick up my diary.

## BAD TIMING

At that moment, the telephone rang. The men told me to answer it. "Answer it and pretend that everything's normal"! They said. There were now two guns pointed at either side of my head. Thank God for my speech and drama training! I was able to answer the phone with a relatively normal tone of voice. It was the CEO of the company, who was calling from Johannesburg to speak to Charles. Because I had never answered the phone before, the CEO began asking me questions, such as "Who are you and why are you there"? The robbers were becoming increasingly anxious as I continued to respond to, what seemed like hundreds of the CEO's questions. Finally, the CEO asked to speak to Charles. I knew, though, that Charles was in no state to speak to him. In fact, he wasn't even close by. The robbers had him on the ground, with his hands tied behind his back, and a gun to his head.

"Charles cannot come to the telephone", I said. "He has gone to the bathroom".

"Well, get him to call me back", said the CEO.

"I will", I replied and hung up. I was very relieved as I was terrified during the call.

The two men holding me at gunpoint pushed me to the safe. It's only by the grace of God that the safe opened the first time I tried! The men swung the door of the safe wide open to reveal a huge sum of money. (Incidentally, I had written a report about a week prior to this robbery which stated that there were several risks in the business and that one of these risks was that many of the employees were aware that there was a lot of cash received each day and that there was a safe on the premises).

Due to their heightened fear, the robbers were swearing violently, which added to the tension considerably. It was mayhem. After the robbers emptied the safe, they asked me for my handbag. They took my cell phone and my wallet.

They asked Charles for his cell phone and took his wallet. Then they asked me for my car keys, which I gave them. They told me to lie down on the ground and threatened, "If you move, we'll kill you".

## DIVINE PROTECTION

At this stage, my fear was escalating because I realized that the other employees would soon be arriving and, if they interrupted the robbery, the robbers would panic and there would be bloodshed. I never stopped praying...not for a second. I was lying on the floor face to face with Charles who was in an abysmal state. All the while, the robbers were swearing at us and yelling, "If you move, we will kill you"! We were petrified.

Things quietened down. We listened intently for any indication that could assure us that the robbers had got what they were coming for and fled the scene. I indicated to Charles not to move. A couple of minutes passed without us hearing a sound. Those terrible minutes dragged on like hours, to coin a cliché.

Finally, we were confident the danger had passed. We looked at each other and realised that we had made it out alive and unscathed. Charles said, "I don't know what you have that kept you so calm and composed, but I want what you have". I told him that I am nothing in my own strength and that what I have is faith in God. I witnessed to him then and there about the power of God and believing in our Lord Jesus Christ. Right there, as we lay on the floor with our faces in the dust and dirt, I brought him to the Lord. Glory be to God!

## SILVER LINING

Needless to say, I resigned immediately after the robbery because I knew I was at huge risk in terms of security.

Charles's acceptance of God in his life was wonderful. I have yet to hear how his Christian adventure went after the robbery, but I hope and trust that he stayed committed to understanding and relying upon the power and presence of God in his life.

But there was another blessing from this experience. Beautiful Voice and I began to date.

# Paul

*I have yet to hear a man ask for advice on how to combine marriage and a career.*

—Gloria Steinem

**PAUL BOTES AND** I dated for three wonderful years. He was my greatest champion, ally and fan as I climbed the proverbial workplace ladder, but once I had achieved the CEO position of the *United Business Women* (UBW), things changed.

Paul didn't like the fact that there was so much media attention focused on me. After eight months of me being CEO, he said he wanted me to leave my position and join him in his business. I would spend weekends supporting him in his business, but I couldn't stop working and earning. I am very independent and I knew he couldn't support us both as his business was not profitable yet.

In August that year, I orchestrated the biggest and most important event of my career. The media was intent on me that night because my guest speaker was the new Deputy President of the country. It was an extremely sensitive time in the political history of the country, and she had just come into power. You can imagine the heavy security and press that were at this function! As CEO, I was the go-to person and, because I knew I'd be working, I had asked Paul not to attend.

"I'll be completely occupied seeing to my guests. There will be over a thousand people attending, including my branch coordinators who are flying in from all over the country, UBW members, sponsors and VIPs. I won't have a moment to sit with you and relax", I said.

Paul insisted on attending. He despised all the attention I received that night and walked out halfway through the ceremony. I never saw him again.

# Rage

*Rage—whether in reaction to social injustice, or to our leaders' insanity, or to those who threaten or harm us—is a powerful energy that, with diligent practice, can be transformed into fierce compassion.*

—Bonnie Myotai Treace

**A COUPLE OF** months after that first robbery, I was fast asleep in the townhouse that I shared with my son, Eric, when a noise woke me up. I heard it again and knew immediately that we were being burgled. But this time, I wasn't the least bit frightened. Rather, I was angry...furious, in fact. I felt no fear whatsoever, which was really stupid.

For a two week period after being held at gunpoint, I had been very anxious and apprehensive. The company had offered to pay for me to go for therapy, but I didn't have time and I knew they'd only pay for one or two sessions. My anxiety dispersed, though, as I focused on running my drama school and I felt as if I had healed from the trauma. But now, being robbed in my own home, coupled with all the rage pent up from the first robbery, I was blinded to reason and logic as I listened to the robbers talking and moving about on the other side of my bedroom wall.

### GREEK BLOOD

I went berserk. I often laugh about the fact that my temper, once sparked, can go from naught to one hundred in a split second. I often refer to this as having 'real Greek blood in my veins'. And this is exactly what happened. I opened my bedroom door and grabbed a walking stick, which had belonged to my late grandmother. What I was going to do with this walking stick, I really didn't know, but that's the stupidity of the rage that consumed me. I went to the door of the room the perpetrators were in and could hear them speaking to one another, but I couldn't understand them. They were speaking Fanagolo, a colloquial language that most tribes understand. I was slightly familiar with the language from my days in Zululand, but I was too anxious to listen and decipher what was being said. The burglars were rummaging through my cupboards. I heard them open my car door, as well, which I never used to lock because my garage had a security system. But they had forced the garage door open to gain access to the house.

### GRANDMOTHER'S WALKING STICK

As my cupboards were being raided, I took my grandmother's walking stick and hammered on the door with all my might. I screamed and shouted and swore at the marauders. I screeched at them to get out because the police were coming.

When the walking stick broke through the first layer of wood on the door and got stuck, I began pounding on the door with my knuckles. Eric, who was twenty-one years old at the time, woke and, by the time he reached me, the knuckles on my right hand were stripped of skin and bleeding profusely.

I continued to scream. "Phone the police! Phone the police! Phone the police"! Poor Eric had no idea what was going on. I yelled, "Right in there, they're robbing us, in there"! Eric, being logical, forced me away from the door, knowing that the looters could shoot through the door and kill me.

## QUIET AGAIN

Things got quiet. My screams and pounding had frightened the robbers away. We found a firearm that one of them had dropped in his hurry to exit the garage and a trailer packed with items they had burgled from my neighbors.

The local police station was only two blocks away from the townhouse complex, and the police arrived very quickly. The neighbors heard the sirens and came around to see what was happening. Needless to say, they were thrilled to retrieve all of their items intact.

The irony is that all my neighbors had dogs, but not a single dog had barked during any of the burglaries. Evidently, I had done all the barking.

## GREAT THERAPY

Given that my four immediate neighbors each had a dog that sleeps inside and yet none of them heard the robbers, I do believe that God woke me up to save me from who knows what, and I give Him all the glory. I know that it was foolish to proceed without caution. Weeks later, I heard Eric telling his friends who were concerned over him being fearful, "No guys, I'm not scared of being burgled. I'm scared of my mother's reaction".

My knuckles healed, although I do still suffer with sore knuckles in the cold weather. The rage I felt and expressed was my therapy. It released all the anger I had for the first robbery and healed me.

# Intuition Calls It

*In a time of universal deceit, telling the truth is a revolutionary act.*

—George Orwell

**WHEN I BECAME** CEO of United Business Women (UBW), the UBW president, who was not an executive, but rather the figurehead of the organization, informed me that she, along with a very prominent business woman and a political leader's wife, wanted to host the world's first social entrepreneurship conference under the auspices of UBW.

I had a bad feeling about this conference from the very beginning. First off, the board needed to know and to give the president a mandate. She had concocted this idea over the Christmas holidays and nobody was told of her scheme. She tried to sell me on the idea, but my intuition, my experience and I weren't buying it. All my alarm bells were going off. She said they had a date and were planning this conference with less than four months to prepare. I knew that a conference of this magnitude takes at least two years to plan properly.

## Intelligent Questions Not Allowed

Many planning sessions ensued with whom could arguably be considered the six most powerful women in the country. Every time I asked an intelligent question, I was shut down. They responded to my questions by belittling and embarrassing me.

I asked, "Do you have a budget? Do you have a team that can implement your plan? What about IT solutions for real-time registration"?

The most applauded of all the women who also was chairman of one of the biggest corporations in the world said, "Yes, of course"!

When I asked where the funding was going to come from, I was told that they could raise millions of rands in a couple of days. I felt, "Who am I, little Tina Thomson, questioning these powerful women who have done it all before"? But my intuition, my gut feel, my Holy Spirit, kept stabbing me. They kept saying, "Tina, this is a disaster in the making".

During the next six weeks, not one of these powerful women was ever on time to our meetings. Every meeting, I arrived on time with a file filled with my concerns and questions, but the other women negated my concerns and deflected my questions by emphasising that they knew what they were doing, and I did not.

## Conference Eve

The wife of the political leader had arranged for conference bags to be purchased to the tune of R250,000-00. The bags were to be delivered to the conference center the night before the conference for me and my staff to fill with conference documents. But only half of the bags arrived, and they were poorly constructed of shoddy burlap, with safety pins holding the beadwork instead of the bags being beaded. I was horrified.

## An Utter Disaster

The conference was a complete disaster. To fill the seats, the so-called six most powerful women in the country - the 'conference planners', decided to bus disadvantaged women in, with the promise of a free meal. I was beyond embarrassed. The plenary sessions were sparsely attended and, of the people who did attend them, very few could contribute. The conference ended, leaving massive debt in its wake.

I had forewarned my board, often and in writing that "the conference was a disaster in the making". Throughout the planning process, I had sent several emails to my board to let them know that I was not happy endorsing the conference, that I did not approve of it, and warned them to pull out. Believe me, I can make a big stink about things of which I don't approve.

## Bag Lady

The governmental department that promised some funding to the UBW president did not come through for her. I was not surprised. The wife of the political leader made an effort to raise some funds by holding an exclusive, expensive breakfast at the State House, but the amount raised was insufficient to pay the vendors. As funds were allocated, the creditors were paid.

These same six powerful women decided that I should be the one to manage all incoming donations and funds, and pay the creditors. One of these creditors was the woman who had made the conference bags. As she never did deliver the remainder on the order, the Bag Lady was moved to the bottom of the list of creditors.

One day, the Bag Lady showed up at my office with three henchmen. As these enormous men entered the office, my personal assistant saw them and her tone alarmed me. I could not see the external door of the office from where I sat, but then I saw my second in command, who was a lady of color, turn snow white, and I knew that something was wrong.

As I got up and moved around my desk, I prayed. I prayed that God would protect my people and me, and that I would have the authority in Jesus's name to protect us.

What unfurled next was not due to my own strength. I stepped up to one of the huge men. He said, "We've come for the money for the bags". I looked up at the henchman and told him, "You go to the people who signed your order and you ask them for the money. I played no part in this".

The Bag Lady stepped forward. She name dropped the most prominent woman's name and title and said, "...she has sent us and she said that you will pay us", she said.

I felt no fear whatsoever, as I was filled with the power and bravery of the Holy Spirit, and retorted, "You tell her to pay you. She and the wife of the political leader hired you, and this has nothing to do with me or with the UBW"!

"The President of this organisation told us to come here to get the money", she shouted.

"You go and you tell the president that she is a figurehead, but I am the executive of this organisation. I am the custodian of our members' money and I'm telling you right now to get the hell out of my office"!

Well, they turned around, those three thugs and their queen (who resembled a witch doctor). They turned right around and filed out of the office. Only after I closed the door behind them did the horror of the situation sink in. My people were shaken and in shock, so I sent them home to recover. And I fell to my knees in gratitude.

# A Colossal 2008

*If we had no winter, the spring would not be so pleasant: if we did not sometimes taste of adversity, prosperity would not be so welcome.*

—Anne Bradstreet

**A LOT HAPPENED** in 2008 throughout the world. For me, the drama was all within a six-week period…the first of April to the fourteenth of May, to be exact.

During those six weeks, I experienced three momentous catastrophes. The first and weightiest was when Eric left South Africa for a job in the United States. The second major blow was that I both fell in love and broke up with a phenomenal man, whom I adored and trusted. And the third disaster happened when I started a new job and discovered horrific corruption within the organization on my second day in.

It would have been challenging enough if these incidents happened one at a time but, as is so often the case in life, they did not. Rather, they ran concurrently, which made my life traumatic everywhere and all at once. Yes, 2008 was unbelievably challenging.

## MOTHER AND CHILD

Few people understood my son's and my close relationship. We were the best of friends and had been through many crises together. We had purchased a home together as equal business partners, and spent a lot of time together visiting friends and family, traveling, going to the movies and dining out. All of Eric's friends and girlfriends understood the importance of his mother to him. Eric was, and is, my life.

When Eric was headhunted and offered a job in the U.S., I was thrilled for him. I wanted the best for Eric. The day Eric was to leave for the US drew near. He had many farewell parties with friends and family. His things were packed, and he was ready to go. Everything was happening so fast! But once he boarded the plane on the twenty-seventh of April, the reality of his relocation hit me. I was surprised at how traumatic it was to part from my son.

## ANDREW

Earlier that month of April, my close friend and confidant, Andrew, turned forty. I met Andrew when I joined the company for which he worked. The CEO had created a unique position for me and, in order to place me in the right department, had positioned me as reporting to Andrew. The CEO had made it very clear, though, that we were peers. An extraordinarily handsome man nine years younger than me and a womaniser, Andrew often regaled me with his escapades and always asked my advice. We worked together for ten months and had a superb professional relationship. After I left the company, Andrew wrote me a glowing letter of reference. He often emailed me to say he missed me and that the place wasn't the same without me.

I also knew Andrew's sister, Joan, and his sister-in-law, Debbie. They were throwing a fortieth birthday party for him two weeks before Eric's departure and they decided to invite me as a surprise for Andrew. The only other outsider invited was Andrew's best friend and his best friend's wife. I had an uneasy feeling that there was a hidden agenda regarding my inclusion in the festivities, but couldn't peg it. Andrew was his characteristically charming and wonderful self throughout the evening. I also noticed, though, that everything Andrew said about and to me during the celebration was ambiguous. I couldn't grasp what was really going on, but I had a lovely time and figured that it was good for me to have fun instead of being anxious about Eric's pending departure.

### A Different Kind of Hug

A few days later, Andrew invited me to dinner. We had shared many breakfasts and lunches when we worked together, but being invited to dinner felt a little different. Again I had the niggling feeling that there was something going on with Andrew that I wasn't privy to. We had been in almost daily communication, due to my calling him for legal advice regarding my whistleblowing at WCH (Women Change History)

Andrew picked me up for dinner and we had a fabulous time. When he returned me home, he walked me inside and wished Eric "all the best" in his new adventure in the U.S. Then we hugged goodbye, as we had always done, but this hug felt very different...

### A Cherished Custom

April twenty-seventh, the day Eric was to leave for the U.S., arrived. Eric and I have had an ongoing custom that when either one of us boards a plane, the other would telephone to say, "Goodbye and Godspeed". But, after Eric and I had parted at the airport, I realized that I had lost my cell phone along the way. I was frantic. With a little bit of time before his plane departed and crying uncontrollably, I got in my car, raced home, and made it in record time. I dashed to my landline, called Eric, and was able to speak with him for a few minutes before takeoff.

### A Six Week Wonder

After I hung up with Eric, I called Andrew sobbing. Andrew, who is a phenomenal parent and an extremely caring person, knew that being apart from Eric was going to be painful for me, and he had planned to visit me when Eric left. Bear in mind that Andrew is extraordinarily handsome, charming and comforting. Also, that I was extremely vulnerable. Our relationship changed. I don't regret what happened.

We had an amazing relationship, but one that was probably doomed from the outset. At the time, Andrew was traveling to another province every other weekend to see his children. Also, his ex-wife had a hold on him, so he complied with all her demands, even when it took him away abruptly from work and from me.

It just wasn't working. After six weeks, we broke up. The breakup was so heart wrenching for me, that I did not have another relationship for almost seven years afterward. There were times that I thought our relationship might be rekindled. In September 2009, when I returned from my fiftieth birthday party in Greece, Andrew asked me to give it another try, but we both realized that doing so would be unwise.

During one of our last conversations, I counselled Andrew to find a younger woman with no children of her own, so she could attend to his own children…a woman who could adapt to his lifestyle, and then to marry her. He took my advice and, one year later, became a happily married man. With great respect for Andrew and what we had, I never contacted him ever again. I do stay in contact with his sister and sister-in-law, however, both of whom are dear to me, and so I know that he is well. For several years, I stayed in contact with his teenage daughter, too, but realized later that it was time to cut all ties.

Andrew is a phenomenal man. And such a good soul! To this day, I have no doubt that if Andrew ever needed me, I would help him…and I'm bold enough to say that would apply vice versa. I wish God's richest blessings upon him. While the breakup was painful, it's good we did not continue. What we had was very precious!

### EXCITED TO HELP THE COUNTRY'S WOMEN ENTREPRENEURS

I got my entrée into government when I was CEO of the largest and most credible women's organization in the country. The government had a department that advanced women entrepreneurs called WCH, (Women Change History) and as CEO of the largest women's organisation, I was expected to serve as Vice Chairman of the Board of WCH that in turn represented the many groups of women's organisations in the country.

### ALL TALK, NO SHOW

I always promote collaboration. As CEO of the very visible women's organization, I frequently invited the heads of the WCH to my organisation's events. It was plain to see that that WCH lacked structure and leadership. Partnering with them was always chaotic. Meetings were a nightmare. From the get-go, I could see that they were incapable of delivering on anything. I also could see that they had a very strong foundation and the potential to be an effective organization. Their acting CEO (although she was never given the full position) also served as the Director of another unit in the department.

## Seeking a Diversion

When I had exited the UBW, The Chairman of WCH's board approached me several times to work for WCH. She was quite insistent. Her timing was right. My own circumstances impelled me to pay attention to her offer. I was facing big changes. My executive role with another company was neither rewarding nor challenging. And my son was about to leave home for the U.S. I needed a diversion.

I also knew some of the challenges that lay ahead with WCH, as I had experienced them firsthand when I was CEO. During my interview with WCH's Board, I said, "I am well aware of the problems and will need autonomy, if I am going to turn WCH around and clean it up". As a turnaround specialist, I was confident that I could help the organisation become successful. My contract read that I'd have a full mandate to do whatever it took to make the organization successful.

However, the board also told me that it simply would not work for a white woman to be 'officially' in charge of WCH. I understood completely. As they needed WCH's CEO to be of a woman of color, the acting CEO would continue as head of WCH. I don't care about titles and this was fine with me. I had a lot of work to do to get this organization working for the women of my beloved country.

Excited for the women of South Africa, I decided to devote myself to WCH for two years. I believed in WCH's potential to accomplish great things for women countrywide and was looking forward to helping build its success and scalability. I would have my own office and staff in Johannesburg, while the acting CEO would continue to work out of Iliwa.

Little did I know what horrors lay ahead.

## Ma'am, My Ass

Nothing could have prepared me for what I discovered on my second day of work for WCH. My receptionist told me that "Ma'am", an appellative that signifies respect and one that the acting CEO did not deserve, requested that she go to Iliwa for the day. Because I was still setting up my office and didn't have a lot of work for her to do, I consented. At the end of the day, the receptionist returned from Iliwa with an invoice for me to sign.

"What is this"? I asked.

She replied that it was for the car service she had used during her day in Iliwa, where she had been required to do *Ma'am's* grocery shopping, pick her children up from school and take them to their grandmother's, and drop the groceries off at *Ma'am's* house, before being driven back to Johannesburg. I had to hold my chin to stop my jaw from dropping and asked my receptionist to leave the invoice with me.

"No", she said. "Ma'am said to have you sign it and then I should return it to her tonight".

I did not want to shoot the messenger, nor did I want to explain the wrongness of *Ma'am's* actions to her. I told her that I would not sign the invoice and requested again that she leave it with me. She picked up the invoice and left my office. Moments later, my phone rang. It was 'the boss' wanting to know why I wouldn't sign the invoice when she had already approved it.

"I will not countersign the invoice! You are not entitled to use government property and taxpayers' money, for your personal use", I said.

"Just sign it", she said. "You will quickly see how things are done around here."

I did not sign it.

Two days later, "Ma'am" visited me in my Johannesburg office. She tried to convince me that what she had done was above board, but to no avail. It was wrong. I refused to pander to her. Everything went to hell from there, as I began to uncover the depth of her illicit behavior.

## The Plot Sickens

I quickly gained the trust of my employees. By week four, they were sharing with me all the things that *Ma'am* had forced them to do. One of my staff members was a young man with a post graduate degree whom I admired greatly for his character and integrity.

I said to him, "You keep telling me that you were forced to submit invoices to Treasury for "Ma'am's" personal expenses. How did she force you"?

"Mrs. Thomson, the very first time she asked me to submit a request to Treasury for something I knew was false, I refused. She said I should write that the funds were to provide a workshop for the women in one of the rural towns, but I knew that they were really for a luxury bus to take her family to a wedding", he said, his eyes filling with tears.

*Ma'am's* response to his refusal was to look him in the eye and threaten to harm his children, if he did not comply.

"I know where your children go to school", she said.

At this point, I patted his arm and reassured him that that was enough. While I had heard of this type of thing happening, to encounter it firsthand was shocking. I had to eradicate this evil. I had to free these people who were under this terrible, terrible tyranny and had been for three or four years before I had taken the reigns. I have very few fears and whistle blowing isn't one of them. I've come to learn that evil can be conquered when someone takes a stand for what is right.

## Danger

I gathered as much evidence as possible to include in my report to the Board. At the end of my first month with WCH, I submitted my report. The days that followed were eerily silent. No one responded. So I asked for a meeting.

The meeting was bizarre. I was stunned to see *Ma'am* in attendance. The Board Members justified everything she had done, even though I had documentation to substantiate her wrongdoing. With the support of her Board, this tyrant rationalized her actions and made it seem as if I were in the wrong and being "condescending", a word she threw in several times.

But I wasn't going to stop there. I sent my report to as many people as possible, with the hope that someone somewhere would investigate. One week after I sent out my report, a trusted advisor called me.

"Are you crazy? The woman you're accusing is literally in bed with the leader of the department. In fact, he is the father of her child. Do not do this, Tina, you're in danger".

That didn't stop me either.

## MUTI

In my sixth week with WCH, the new Tea Lady placed a cup of coffee on my desk as I was entering the office. One of my loyal staff members saw this and ran into my office, flinging the cup to the floor.

"Don't touch that, Mrs. Thomson! That has *muti* in it". (*Muti* is derived from the Zulu word for medicine, generally used by witch doctors).

"Really?" I asked, wondering if it were possible that my coffee had been poisoned.

My staff member explained that the week prior, Telkom (the telecommunications monopoly in South Africa) came to "inspect" the wiring, but she was convinced that they were really bugging the office. She then pointed out that, all of a sudden, we got a new Tea Lady. Nepotism ran rampant in the government so, while on one hand, such notions seemed far-fetched, on the other, they were scarily believable. I called Andrew, my friend and confidant, who is an expert in labour practice.

"Get out of there", he said. "You need to go and go fast".

I still wasn't sure, but decided to go home for the day. When I reached my car in the parking garage, one of my tyres had been slashed. I had the tyre repaired but, instead of going home, I drove straight to Iliwa.

I marched straight into *Ma'am's* office and right up to her until we were only a few inches apart, face-to-face.

"I've had enough! I'm out of here but I'm onto you!" I shouted, along with a few choice words.

Then I went to my car and called the Chairman of the Board. "I'm not giving any notice. I'll write you an official letter of resignation, but I am out of here".

I was advised to hire a bodyguard and to hide until I was safe, since the story had reached a few of the people who had been reading all my emails and reports. I took the advice.

## A GOOD ENDING

The investigation took two years. All the staff members were interrogated and subpoenaed. And all but one were cleared of any wrongdoing. Not all the Board Members were cleared, however. *Ma'am* was suspended and, ultimately, fired. The people who worked for this tyrant are free now and most of them stayed in their jobs. One of my colleagues, a senior financial executive, who was hired around the same time as I was, had been instrumental in helping the forensic auditors complete their investigation. Shirley I salute you!

Although this experience cost me three months' salary and, in the process I lost my home, I would do it all again.

## RESILIENT

Between Eric moving to the U.S., falling deeply in love and then breaking up with Andrew, and whistleblowing at

WCH, I had been traumatised and was depressed. I couldn't stop crying. I cried about anything and everything. When my weeping continued for several weeks, I sought help from Dr. Robert Graham, the same doctor who delivered Eric twenty-seven years prior. He ran a series of tests for depression. The results showed that I was not clinically depressed, but that my depression was due to circumstances. For six months, I took a very low dosage of an antidepressant until I was on terra firma once again.

Yes, the beginning of 2008 was traumatic in many respects. But I survived. I bounced. And by September, I was thriving.

# If The Name Fits

*It ain't what they call you, it's what you answer to.*

—W.C. Fields

**I MET JOHN** Thomas when his firm, Telos, offered me a six-month contract. After whistleblowing at WCH and my subsequent unemployment, I desperately needed the work and was profoundly grateful for the opportunity.

I realised that Telos wanted me for my trusted network. I had successfully completed extensive research when I conducted a *Leadership Census* in 2005 and 2006. The data sample for the research included every company listed on the Stock Exchange, as well as the seventeen biggest state-owned enterprises. The census methodology required that I speak with the CEO of each of the three-hundred-sixty-two companies. Telos knew my reputation and that I had a goldmine of contacts, and they gave me the job. Thank God!

John, Founder and Managing Director of Telos, was a handsome and distinguished looking man. And he knew it. John was also a male chauvinist. It bothered him greatly that I knew as many or, perhaps, even more influential people than he did and that I had personal contact with many of them. This competition with me didn't make sense, given that it was in his best interest for me to make those connections and be able to acquire those clients for Telos.

I didn't realize what I was up against until one night when John introduced me as "the previous leader of the suffragettes", mocking my having been CEO of United Business Women (UBW). From that time on, I knew that John would try to bully me. There is justice, however. The person to whom he had introduced me as "the previous leader of the suffragettes" was a journalist who had interviewed me a couple of times in the past and knew me. She replied, "Oh, of course I know Tina Thomson, she is amazing."

Then she grabbed me and walked off, leaving him standing alone at the function. John resented the fact that people knew and liked me.

### John Thomas?

I was uncomfortable using the name "John Thomas". When I grew up, "John Thomas" referred to a penis. It's often used in regards to little boys, such as, "Put your John Thomas away" or "Wash your John Thomas". Nothing in me could call my managing director "John Thomas". So I always referred to him as "Mr. Thomas"

The directors told me that he did have some long, drawn-out name, but that he was known, professionally and otherwise, as "John Thomas" and did not like being called anything else. I, however, continued to call him "Mr. Thomas".

### Mr. Thomas Intrudes

One day, Mr. Thomas called me into his office. He had seen my electronic calendar and took note that I had an appointment scheduled with the CFO of a large oil company.

She was a woman with whom I was very well acquainted from my previous work with the UBW. I had also served on a judging panel for successful women and had recently evaluated and awarded her.

I entered Mr. Thomas's office.

"I see that you're going to see this individual in two days. I'm going with you", he said.

"Mr. Thomas, please don't come with me", I implored. "She is an associate, not a friend. I need to inform her that I am working for Telos now. I'm meeting with her to plant a seed, not to go in to headhunt her nor to ask her to hire us to fill the positions in her department".

Not caring a bit, he interrupted me and said, "I'm going with you". He then interrupted me for a second time and said, "And I want you to start using my first name and surname – none of this 'Mr. Thomas' anymore".

I just stared at him.

"It's not correct for me to use your first name. You are my CEO and managing director," I said.

But John Thomas would have none of it and said, "You must use my full name, especially when you introduce me".

## FAUX PAS

Lo and behold, the day of my appointment with the CFO arrived. Mr. Thomas called me over the intercom.

"I'll see you at my car," he said.

The ride to the meeting was uncomfortable. I felt as if Mr. Thomas were treating me like a child and that the "Big Boss" was going with me to the appointment to make sure that it went well. I was anxious as to how my associate would accept Mr. Thomas's presence. But there was nothing I could do. En route to the meeting, I tried to focus and repeatedly told myself to stay calm and be professional. I decided that I would contact my associate afterwards and apologise.

As we approached her plush office, she stood up and walked towards us. And, then, *it* happened. In my nervousness, I introduced John Thomas as "Tom Johnas". He was horrified, but didn't say anything. For the rest of the meeting, my associate called him "Mr. Johnas".

# A Glorious 50th

*The more you praise and celebrate your life, the more there is in life to celebrate.*

—Oprah Winfrey

**I TURNED FIFTY** on an island I call 'Paradise' surrounded by my loved ones. It was a dream come true and an exceedingly joyous time. It was also the first time that my beloved son had been to the island of our forefathers. He loved it. I had invited family and friends from across the world to join me. Sadly, my sister and her family were unable to make the trip, but she made a huge effort to be a part of the celebration and surprised me with a memorable and treasured gift of a fabulous party two nights after the big party. She had arranged a local musician to arrive at the party and serenade me on his piano accordion. It was sublime. We danced and my Aunt Sophia cooked all her legendary dishes. My precious sister gifted me an experience I cherish.

The actual day of my birthday was celebrated with a traditional meal at a little taverna on the beach. It was simple and exactly what I wanted.

The third party—oh yes, the celebration continued for a week—took place aboard the Eftychía, a gorgeous boat owned by my dearest friends, Dennis and Athena. I had not, in my wildest dreams, imagined that I would be treated to another party, let alone on a yacht in the magnificent waters that embrace the shores of picturesque Paradise island! Dennis and Athena had invited my immediate family to join us for dinner in the charming village across the channel, on the neighbouring island.

A few of my relatives had never been on a yacht and it was a delight to see them enjoying the adventure. There were squeals of disbelief as Athena emerged from the kitchen with local and Swiss delicacies. I overheard my seventy-six-year-old aunt say, "This is just like the movies". Her clichéd words described the scene aptly. The weather was perfect and the azure blue sea was awe-inspiring. Our senior guests were astounded at how comfortable and spacious the yacht was. For several summers, they had seen Eftychía anchored in the bay, but had no idea that the 'boat under the canvass shade-cloth' was so well-appointed. I shall not relate the gleeful remarks that were passed after visiting the bathroom!

It was on this return trip to Ithaca at one o'clock in the morning that I realised my dream had come true. Our guests were all very quiet and mellow, partly from the sumptuous meal and largely from the local wines, a huge contrast from the excited chatter on the way over. I was completely sober and went to sit on the edge of the deck all alone.

The stillness of the night, with its almost-full moon reflecting on the water, was overwhelming. I felt so fulfilled and so blessed. But there was more. For a grand finale, Athena turned on Andrea Bocelli's *Romanza* full volume and flooded the night with sweetness, a moment which will forever remain etched in my heart and soul. *This* was happiness.

This birthday celebration replenished, revitalized and restored me. Two of Eric's birthday gifts to me were an exquisite Burberry handbag and scarf. And then, to top it off, he gave me a trip with him to New York City over Christmas. What a dream!

# New York

*I have found that if you love life, life will love you back.*

—Arthur Rubenstein

**ERIC AND I** travelled to New York for Christmas 2009. He had returned temporarily to South Africa in December 2008, but I knew he loved New York and it was a matter of time before he returned. Out of all my travels the world over, this trip stands out as the best of my life. We had three-and-a-half weeks of absolute bliss. I have never laughed so much…ever. I felt such freedom. Each day was overflowing with magical moments. No words can express how grateful I am to Eric for this extraordinary gift.

Eric had lived in New York the previous year and it was wonderful to see firsthand all the spots that he had shared with me in word pictures and photos over email. We laughed our way through the city. I mean doubled-over, gasping-for-air, pants-wetting laughter! Memories of this vacation with Eric have been lifesavers during dark times.

Christmas day was a real treat. Long time dear friends,

Roger, and his wife, Cristina, opened their home to us and prepared a feast. There was much merriment and special moments.

Another precious gift I received in New York on Christmas day was the meeting of a very old soul, a man whom I will love forever... but this is a story for another time...

# No Grey Areas

*We leave our handprints on everything we touch. Long after the print fades, the impression they made lasts forever.*

—Samantha Storsberg

**I NEVER HAVE,** nor will I ever, sacrifice my integrity for anyone or anything. There have been many times when I truly needed the money and, if I had been willing to step into a grey area, I would be wealthy now. But I refuse to go *there.* The price is too high.

## BETRAYAL

I found myself in a very difficult situation at the beginning of my coaching business. I had trusted the man who taught me all there was to know about executive coaching. I partnered with him on some projects. He was a brilliant coach and I subscribed to his methodology. But he went behind my back and approached one of my trusted advisors, the chairman of a large corporation in South Africa, to pitch our coaching services. Jerry, my business partner (someone she didn't know);

blatantly told her, "Tina said you would speak to us". And he neglected to tell me what he had done, because he knew it was wrong. It was completely out of line for him to do so. I should have been the one to approach her and ask if there were any way she could introduce me to her HR Director.

My advisor relayed the incident to me. She asked me, "Why didn't you come to me directly, rather than asking Jerry to do this"? I was appalled and very embarrassed! I was also furious! I explained to her that I had no knowledge of Jerry's actions and that I did not want to work for her organisation or I would have asked her myself. I felt that working for her company would have been an unfair advantage, as people knew that I was friendly with her. I wanted to sign business on merit and not on whom I know. I had integrity. Jerry didn't. I broke off the partnership with him immediately and never worked with him again.

### Doing What I Do Best and Letting Go of the Rest

Soon after the incident with Jerry, a South African listed company asked me to coach one of their senior executives whom they had targeted for a promotion. The senior executive, Sam, did not understand that coaching is an enormous privilege, an investment made by the company in an individual to take them from good to great.

Sam entered the room and sat down. With his arms belligerently crossed in front of him, he asked me, "What qualifies you to coach me"? Immediately, I realized that he had misunderstood the Board's gesture and did not understand what coaching was. I spent the next hour giving him some case studies of how coaching supports individuals and how effective it was for executives. I am an Executive Coach who has experienced the benefits of coaching firsthand when I was a CEO, so I shared with him the great gain I had derived from coaching. I was transparent with him about some of my most valuable moments being coached, and how my mentors and coaches had supported me through many crises.

My client began to relax. I always coach for one and a half hours. The first half hour is very necessary to allow time for the client to talk about personal matters, offload and settle down. Sam needed the full session to be at ease. I didn't mind.

The second session went better, because he had begun to develop trust in me. After forty-five minutes, he started to share very personal matters with me. I listened carefully and asked him questions that drew him out further. He left, saying that he "enjoyed" our coaching session.

Our third session followed a similar pattern. As much as I tried to focus the conversation on his work, I could not get him off the personal stuff. I tried all sorts of things, but nothing worked. I was keenly aware that I had been contracted for a six-month period to help Sam to develop leadership skills to drive his team to deliver on their strategy. At the end of our third session, I said to him, "Next week, we must focus on work issues. I appreciate knowing more about you personally and your situation at home, but I am contracted to be your *executive* coach". He assured me that he would be ready to focus on work the following week.

Meanwhile, I sought advice from experts and other coaches. They advised me that I had approached the situation correctly and had done all I could do.

During our fourth session, I battled in vain to get him to focus on work. Afterwards, I went to his CEO and said that I needed to cancel the contract, and that what Sam really needed was a therapist. I added that I am neither a therapist, nor a life coach, and that working with this man was out of my frame of reference. The CEO was alarmed. "Please don't withdraw! He is very happy. His team has seen a big change in him. Please! Tina just continue what you are doing".

But I could not continue because I was unable to deliver what I was hired to deliver. In addition, I was unqualified to help him with his personal issues. I cancelled the contract, even though I desperately needed the money. It was 2008 and I had suffered huge financial loss after my whistle-blowing. Not only did I need the income, I needed to build credibility and get experience in my new career. But I wasn't the right person to coach this individual.

Friends' words still ring in my ear.

"Tina, you're shooting yourself in the foot again", they said.

"I will never sacrifice my integrity for anything, let alone for money", I replied.

# My Nairobi Sister

*Sisterhood is powerful.*

—Rosemary Brown

Agnes Grace is the Founder and Managing Director of the A group of Schools in Nairobi, Kenya. After meeting with Agnes briefly, due to my delay when a tree fell across the Mombasa Highway, I knew that I had to meet with her again. She was extraordinary. The following year, 2011, I was going to Nairobi for a conference and planned to visit Agnes whilst I was there. Waiting in the hotel lobby for her driver, I was absolutely stunned to see Agnes walking up the steps. She had come personally with her driver to get me. Our next six hours together affected me greatly. Tears of joy and amazement flowed throughout our afternoon together.

Agnes had a surprise for me. She had arranged to take me to four of her schools and, at each one, the children welcomed me with song, dance, poetry and tributes written especially for me. They had done their research and already knew many things about me. The magnificent children looked at me expectantly and sat in anticipation when Agnes told them that I would address them. I was speechless. I was totally unprepared for so much emotion, but I wanted to seize the opportunity to impart something valuable. I searched the 'wisdom-files' in my head and managed to say a few words whilst trying to not cry. I was presented with gorgeous flowers and handwritten cards. The experience was pure bliss and touched me very deeply.

After visiting the schools, we went to Agnes's home on the Karen Blixen Estate (the original farm from the film, *Out of Africa*, in which Meryl Streep portrayed Danish author Karen Blixen). What a wonderful treat! The view and the luncheon were divine. Agnes is a wise and beautiful woman, and I cherished her every word.

When it was time to go, Agnes walked with me to the car and put her arm around me. Agnes is a very tall woman. I am not. So, towering over me, she put her arm around me and said, "Tina, the next time you come to Nairobi, you must come and stay with me in my house. Please don't go to a hotel. You are my sister". Agnes's sincerity and authenticity, and the honour and happiness that she brought to me that day, will stay with me forever.

# Do All Women Leaders Have A Ph.D?

*Unless all of us are free, none of us will be free.*

—Rosemary Brown

**FOR MANY YEARS,** I'd heard disturbing stories about how women leaders pull other women down, instead of promoting and championing them.

When I was CEO of the *United Business Women*, (UBW), a journalist asked me what I thought that all senior women having a "Ph.D." implied. I didn't know what she meant, so I sidestepped the question and went off on a tangent about women being superbly qualified and equal to men, but not receiving equal pay.

Very quickly after the interview, I tried to research the journalist's question on the Internet, but found nothing. So I asked some seasoned, corporate women leaders what they thought the journalist meant. All of them understood right away. In fact, they couldn't believe that I hadn't heard the "Ph.D." cliché before. They explained that the journalist was referring to "the Ph.D. Syndrome", an acronym for "Pull Her Down". I was horrified.

Obviously, I had experienced the *Pull Her Down Syndrome* to some extent, but because my experience in the corporate world had been with men primarily (I was often the only woman in the room or on a board), I hadn't really experienced the full brunt of this 'syndrome'.

From then on, any time the Ph.D. Syndrome came up, I would vehemently deny its existence and refuse to fan its flames by talking about it. It wasn't until I left the UBW and was approached by *The Magazine* to create a new women-in-business awards process, that I witnessed the Ph.D. Syndrome in all its ugliness...

### A DIFFERENT TYPE OF AWARD

I exited the *United Business Women* (UBW) after two years as CEO and almost four years with the organization. I had started at the bottom, had worked my way up, and had loved it all. One of the CEO's deliverables was to project manage the *Annual Business Awards*, the most prestigious award for women in the country. Those women who are awardees, are titans of industry and have gone on to become legends. I salute them all.

Early the following year, Maura, the founder and owner of a leading *Magazine*, approached me to create an awards process. I declined and told her that it wasn't fair to the UBW; as I didn't want to diminish their *Annual Award*. She persisted, as she felt there was room for other women's awards. We sat down and discussed the issue. I eventually agreed with her. Together, we decided on an awards process that would have completely different aspects than those of The Annual Awards of UBW. We met a couple of times to flesh out the concept. Maura brought her ideas to the table and I honed the process, gave her the dos and don'ts, and came up with five main categories of questions for the questionnaire we'd send to each nominee.

The awards were to be called *The Positively Impactful Women Awards* (PIW). Maura had cleverly decided that we should look at the same twenty-six industries that the *Department of Trade and Industry* classifies, and base the categories of the awards on them. Although she asked me to chair the judging panel that year, I declined out of respect for UBW. I felt it appropriate to wait for a year after my departure from the organisation. By the following year, Maura wanted me as Chair and I accepted.

### CREATING A PIPELINE OF FUTURE LEADERS

It was a great experience to read through the nominations, create a shortlist, and then sit with the judging panel, while they decided upon the winner. Many of the women were phenomenal. However, the nominees in a few of the categories were very weak, so I suggested that we scrap those categories for that year because we didn't want to lower the standard for the award. The judges agreed. However, when we launched the winners to the media, I, as chair of the judging panel, was questioned as to why we scrapped those categories and what we were going to do about it. I explained that the nominees in those categories we dissolved were too weak.

When the journalist persisted and asked, "What are you going to do about it?" I felt I had been given the mandate from Maura to respond on behalf of the award and therefore I went ahead with an idea I had had for a long time.

"What we will do going forward", I said, "is to ask every woman who is nominated for the award to nominate a younger woman in her industry and, in this way, we will create a pipeline of young leaders who could be nominated for the *Positively Impactful Women* award one day".

And that is exactly what we did. In January the following year, the call for nominations in the twenty-six categories defined by the *Department of Trade and Industry* went out throughout the country. It was broadcast in the *Magazine*, the national newspapers, and on the radio. We cast a broad net in order to get the strongest nominations possible of successful women in business and government. We also tweaked the nomination form to include asking each nominee to nominate a younger woman in her industry and explain why she had nominated her. Once the call went out, the nominations began to pour in.

### Reality Check

Six months later, the deadline for nominations had passed and our preliminary panel had begun the examination of the nominations. By the time the judging panel and I, as Chair, sat down to cull the nominations, we had over five hundred qualified nominees. But the harsh reality was that only a few of the nominees had nominated a younger woman in their industry. The fact was that, out of just over five hundred women nominated; only fourteen of them had nominated a younger woman!

I was speechless. In fact, I was close to tears, because everything that I had tried to do to sweep away this scourge of women not supporting other women was happening right in front of my very eyes. It was indisputable. The Ph.D. Syndrome was real. Out of the five hundred plus nominees of female "role models", only fourteen had been willing to nominate a younger woman!

I asked to examine the questionnaire sent to the nominees, because I couldn't believe it. I thought that perhaps there was a mistake or that the question hadn't been clear or perhaps not all of the nominees received the right form. I was incredulous. How could it be possible that so many women were unwilling to nominate a younger woman in their industry?

## CRUSHED

I had to choke back the tears. The lump in my throat returns even now as I write about this. When the questionnaire was brought to me, there it was, as clear as daylight: *Please nominate a younger woman in your industry and give the reason for your nomination.* This was one of our major criteria to qualify the women as being truly eligible for the award. I looked at the judges.

"There are only fourteen valid nominations that meet our criteria and who are on target for this award. We must disqualify the rest", I said emphatically.

There was a deathly silence. We called in Maura, the owner of the award, and I explained the situation to her and strongly recommended that we disqualify the women who had not nominated a younger woman, that women need to promote other women and that, if women don't hold the hands of other younger women, the younger generation of women will be robbed of the experiences and invaluable knowledge that older women are capable of offering them. I told her that all the women in business and government should *want to* pass on their secrets of success and share the ways they handled their ongoing challenges and other valuable lessons. Tragically, this was not the case.

## RIGHT AND WRONG

I was reluctant to continue because, in my world, where there is such clarity as to what is right and what is wrong, it was *wrong* to consider the women who had not nominated a younger woman simply because they hadn't met our criteria. However, I was overruled. There was a majority vote and it was decided that we should go ahead and consider those nominees. I said I would resign as chair of the judging panel. It was wrong to go on with the process.

The judges and Maura did all they could to persuade me to continue. After much deliberation and careful thought, I agreed to continue because disqualifying so many women would appear as though yet another woman's process had failed. Besides, these awards were to showcase women leaders and create role-models for young women.

"If I agree to this and stay on as Chair", I said to Maura, "I must be allowed to highlight this problem. You must allow me to write an article about this issue, and you need to publish the article in your *Magazine*, and, you must allow me extra time in my speaker slot to address the audiences on this topic during the roadshow".

Maura agreed. We proceeded with the judging. And then, as if the heartbreak of women undermining other women were not enough, another symptom of the Ph.D. Syndrome compounded my sadness that day. The nominees' responses to the questionnaire exemplified and substantiated the verity of another stereotype that women in leadership exhibit. A stereotype that I had often addressed in the past and one that I was guilty of myself...

### Typical Woman

As the judges continued to review the completed questionnaires, nomination after nomination of these phenomenal women was ending up in the "no" pile. After the judges had unanimously dismissed five or six extraordinary women in a row, I asked them why these nominees were not being considered. Their answers shared a common thread.

"These women have no substance and haven't achieved much".

Very quickly, I realized that the nominees responded to the questions with wishy-washy-woman answers.

My worst fears were confirmed. Somehow, women did possess a societal design flaw which precluded them from standing up to claim their glory, and acknowledge and celebrate their astounding accomplishments. Their wishy-washy-woman responses screamed of the socialisation of little girls to sit down keep quiet and *don't brag*.

I respect and admire humility, but when women have fundamentally changed the workplace and touched hundreds of lives…when they have significantly affected bottom lines, they do need to stand up and brag. The growing pile of rejected nominees, women who were positively impactful, the cream of the crop and top achievers, distressed me. They simply would not acknowledge and recognize their success, but hid their accomplishments behind modesty which diminished their leadership and the role they played. This was nonsense and this type of thinking had to go.

### Invisible

"My team did this…" or "My team did that…," they wrote. I wanted to shout, "Wake up! Come on. Yes, you're only successful when your team is strong, but you have a strong team only when *you* have led, empowered, and evoked the best out of them. Without your leadership, they couldn't have done it. This is about *you*. *You* have done it. Besides, this is not a lifetime achievement award. This is an award that recognises where you are at this point in time. You've been nominated. Stand up and speak up"!

It is to women's detriment to act invisible.

Naturally, as Chair, I could not interfere with the judging, but I did ask the judges to look deeper into each nominee to see what she has achieved and how she has influenced and mentored others. I also proposed that they do a quick

Google search on each individual.

The responses to our questionnaire shattered my heart. Sadly, I realised that the negative stereotypes about women in leadership were largely true. During the roadshow, I appealed to the women to "stand up".

"Please", I implored, "in the future, please describe everything you've achieved and claim your place as a leader. Quit this conditioning to be modest"!

## DIFFICULT QUESTION

I then asked the finalists, in a very calm monotone, "May I ask why the vast majority of you did not nominate a younger woman"?

You could have heard a pin drop. The audiences during the roadshow ranged between four hundred to a thousand people. Each time I asked the question, the room was dead silent. Many of the women who were finalists and present at those roadshow breakfasts had purchased an entire table for their teams to attend the awards event, and there I was on the stage asking them why they hadn't nominated someone on their team or in their industry. It was awkward and very embarrassing for them. I had arranged to have a photo of a lit candle on the giant screen behind me and I emphasized the wise words, "A candle loses no light when it lights another candle."

During one of the events, two irate, very embarrassed nominees confronted me when I finished speaking. I remained calm and said, "This is neither the time, nor the place. Go back to your office and look at your nomination form. It was a prerequisite to qualify for this award - you had to nominate a younger woman".

Thereafter, I'm proud to say that I proposed, and

witnessed the birth of a mentoring project to develop young women leaders. This was a positive outcome from the debacle I had witnessed. I salute one of my mentors, Fiona, for designing and spearheading this impactful programme run by the Magazine.

# Hot Hot Hot

*Humor is by far the most significant activity of the human brain.*

—Edward De Bono

**THERE HAS ALWAYS** been a warm glow about Athena, which was probably what attracted me to befriend her. We met at the tender age of three years old when we attended Golliwog together. The kindergarten derived its name from Golliwog, a black character in children's books in the late nineteenth century, usually depicted as a type of rag doll. Years later, the school's name was changed, as it was no longer politically correct. But it was called "Golliwog" when Athena and I met and, to this day, we are the best of friends. It's amazing to have such a close friend walk alongside you through every stage of life.

Athena has taught me a lot. One of my favourite stories to relate was how she taught me to 'look older'. When we were in matric, our final year of high school, we traveled to six countries in Europe on a tour organised by our school. There were about sixteen girls on the trip, including our geography teacher. In London, the teacher, along with the rest of the group, wanted to go see the movie, *The Exorcist*. Athena and I both blankly refused. The teacher told us that we had to go and watch the film, because we weren't allowed to be on our own, but we dug in our heels and said, "No way!" We suggested that we could watch the film showing in the movie house next door to the one showing *The Exorcist*. However, the only movie we could see had an age restriction of eighteen and we were only sixteen years old. I, being as short as I am and looking very young at the time, was unlikely to pass for eighteen. So Athena came up with the bright idea that, if I held a cigarette, I would look older and be admitted. She gave me a crash course on how to smoke. She lit the cigarette and handed it to me, and we walked up to the box office. I put on my most mature face and took a puff of the cigarette, trying not to choke, and we managed to buy the tickets.

As we walked towards the door of the movie house, Athena said, "We're early. Let me finish the cigarette before we go in." I then realised that I didn't have the cigarette and had no idea what I had done with it! It was at that point that we smelt something burning. When I reached into my handbag to get my wallet to pay for the ticket, I simply forgot that I had had a cigarette in my hand. The handbag, which was made of burlap, was smoldering. I had to move as fast as lightening to put the fire out because my traveler's checks, passport and airline tickets were in that handbag. When the panic was over, we killed ourselves laughing and I said to Athena, "Well that was quite a lesson on how to smoke, wasn't it"?

### TRAPPED!

In the spring of 2015, Athena visited me in New York for two weeks. Although she had been to visit me the previous year, she had arrived the day of the polar vortex and so we didn't do much walking around my neighbourhood on that trip. This time, I was eager to show her around Bay Ridge, Brooklyn.

On the second day of her visit, we walked to the beautiful Verrazano-Narrows Bridge and around the water's edge. Afterwards, we needed to shop for groceries, as I had waited to shop until Athena arrived, so that she could choose her favorite meals. Off we went to Fantas, a fabulous grocer, in a small, two-story building.

We finished shopping on the ground floor and got into the elevator to go to the second floor with our shopping trolley. We pushed the button for the second floor. The elevator began its ascent, there was an almighty-loud banging noise, and then it stopped.

Athena and I looked at one another. Unbelievable. We pressed practically all the buttons, but the elevator didn't move. When I pressed the alarm to alert someone, a cordial, competent-sounding voice answered immediately and asked what the problem was. I told her we were stuck in the elevator at Fantas in Bay Ridge. She instructed us not to panic and told us that she would send someone immediately. Then she asked if people knew we were in the elevator, to which I replied, "I don't know".

"Well, don't panic", she said, "There is someone on the way".

Ten minutes later, nobody had arrived. Fifteen minutes later, nobody. Athena and I decided that we'd scream and shout and bang on the doors and, hopefully, someone would hear us and realise that we needed help. I pressed the alarm again. Another professional-sounding woman answered and I had to repeat the entire story to her. She said, "Please don't panic. Someone is on their way".

I said, "Look, your colleague told us the same thing twenty minutes ago and nobody has come to our rescue. Nobody seems to know what's going on".

We could hear the shoppers' voices and music playing,

but no one heard us. We heard someone say, "I wonder what's taking the elevator so long". That's when we started to panic. When yet another woman assured us that help was on the way, I asked, "Well, when? How long will they take"? By this stage, we'd been stuck in there for thirty-five minutes.

Four calls later, a lot of expletives and me yelling repeatedly at these stupid people on the other end of the line, "I don't want you to tell me not to panic! I am in a panic! We've been stuck in here for almost an hour!" We started to bang the door as loudly as possible without hurting ourselves. I kicked the door. I hit it with my keys. I hit it with the trolley. I was banging and bashing and thinking we'd be in there forever, because every single woman who answered the phone said, "Don't panic. There's someone on the way". Athena also tried speaking to them. At call number six, I screamed at the woman on the other end, "Where are they coming from and how long will it take"?

"We've just sent someone and they're coming from Staten Island", she replied. I thought I was going to lose it completely. It was rush hour and the trek from Staten Island to Bay Ridge would take at least an hour in the traffic. And so I continued to bang and shout and scream when, all of a sudden, something on the top of the elevator moved.

## Rescue

The elevator roof opened and a man's face peered down at us.

"Ladies, are you all right? Don't panic. We're here to save you", he said.

Athena and I looked at one another quizzically. We weren't sure whether to be relieved, frightened or intrigued.

"No, we are not all right", I said, "We need to get out of here. We're not youngsters. We're old ladies and one of us is ill. We have to get out".

He then explained that he was a fireman and that they'd get us out of there. The manager of Fantas had heard us screaming and pounding on the elevator. But when he phoned the elevator company and was told that their repairman was only leaving Staten Island, already an hour after we had been in the elevator, he knew that we wouldn't be freed for at least another hour and that he could have a problem on his hands if whomever was in the elevator passed out, got ill, or sued the company. Whatever the case may be, he panicked and called the fire brigade.

From then on, it was excruciatingly difficult for Athena and me to contain our laughter. We had the giggles because the fireman on the top of the elevator was extremely serious and very dramatic when he shouted, "Stand back! We're coming down"!

A ladder was lowered into the elevator and down he came. Expecting old ladies, he looked at Athena, who is extraordinarily beautiful, and he looked at me, and he said, "I don't see any old ladies". Athena and I smiled at each other and I said, "Just please get us out of here".

He said, "Right, you're going to go up one at a time. You need to go carefully. You need to hold tight. I have guys at the top who will help you". I let Athena go first. It was a very narrow ladder, the rungs of which were about eight inches wide. Athena climbed up and out. There were five or six pairs of hands at the top helping her. And then it was my turn.

When I got to the top of the ladder, I could no longer stifle my laughter. There were eight firefighters and a group of curious shoppers standing about. When we emerged, we saw that the elevator was actually on the basement floor. When we had heard the loud banging sound, the elevator had dropped, as opposed to going upwards, but we hadn't felt the drop. The climb out of the elevator and up the long elevator shaft out onto the ground floor was hilarious to me. Over and above that, when the firemen had moved the top of the elevator, years of dust accumulation had fallen on us and Athena and I looked like we had survived an explosion of some kind. I found this all very funny.

I had heard how "hot" the firemen were in the U.S. It's true. These young men possessed the most magnificent, statuesque bodies. There Athena and I sat, being attended to by these gorgeous men. They brought chairs for us to sit on and water for us to drink. They were flapping around and fussing over us, making sure we were all right, while the manager of the store, who was quite beside himself, repeatedly asked if we were all right and if he could have our details.

All the while, Athena and I were in agony as we tried to stifle our laughter. We are both South Africans who coped with crises and emergency scenarios as daily occurrences and we could not believe all the drama going on around us simply because of an elevator jam. I couldn't look at Athena at all because I knew that, if we had eye contact, it would be all over. We would come unglued…inappropriate for the occasion.

Then one of the firefighters said to us, "Ladies, you have a guardian angel in the store and there he is"! A man whose job it is to work with elevators had instructed the firefighters how to get into the elevator shaft and lift the top off the elevator, instead of hacking through the steel door to get to us, something they had planned to do. I could not believe this when I heard it. Hack through the steel doors? Wow!

The store manager invited Athena and me to take whatever we needed at no charge, but I said, "Look, we're pretty shaken and very dusty and should go home". Neither Athena nor I knew how much longer we could keep from laughing and we needed to get out of there. He then invited us to return the following day for a Fantas shopping spree, but we did not go. We were too embarrassed. By this stage, we were absolutely famished and, on the short walk home, we decided to go into the Pub to have dinner. Neither of us felt like cooking that night. Besides, we had left Fantas without any groceries.

## THE POSTMORTEM

We were sitting in the Pub after our elevator escapade, when we realized that there had been no cell reception in the elevator and that people might be worried about us. My son, Eric, Athena's husband, Dennis, and their two sons, hadn't been able to reach us for quite some time so, in between fits of laughter, Athena and I decided to check in via Facebook to alleviate their worries. We wrote: "Having a drink after an awful trauma of being stuck in an elevator and being rescued by firemen". You can imagine the responses that post evoked! Some people thought we were kidding, while many others commented that getting stuck in an elevator and being rescued by NY's firefighters was every woman's dream-come-true. We got a lot of comments and chuckled through our meal, trying not to choke with laughter.

We had arranged to meet my friends, Roger and Cristina, for dinner the following night at Embers, a great steakhouse close to my home. Roger has a wonderful sense of humour and he didn't miss the opportunity to start up the conversation by linking "hot firemen, our flames being kindled, and Embers". Naturally, he and Cristina wanted to hear about the "dreadful, traumatic experience" of being stuck in the elevator.

The second that we mentioned Fantas, Cristina almost fainted. She laughed so hard that she was breathless. She is a very gentle, introverted soul and to see her laugh hysterically was extraordinary. She sparked us off and we roared and snorted with laughter. A fellow diner walked across the floor and said, "I've never seen four people laugh so much. Please share the joke".

It took Cristina a good ten minutes before she could speak. She was barely audible because I think she damaged her vocal chords with all the hilarity, but between guffaws she said that she had imagined that we had been in Manhattan, stuck in one of the skyscraper's elevators and that we had to climb up an extremely high elevator shaft. So, it was hilarious to her that we were stuck in the elevator at *Fantas,* a mere two-story building. In fact, Cristina was shopping at *Fantas* just minutes after our rescue and had seen the fuss and wondered what it was all about. When she realized that the large crowd and excessive emergency equipment lying around were related to our rescue, she was uncontrollable with laughter and couldn't eat. And, as is so often the case, sidesplitting laughter is contagious. Athena's sharp sense of humour and the way she related the story to Roger and Cristina was hilarious and contributed significantly to our extreme merriment.

When there was a lull and we could all breathe without bursting into laughter, I told Athena, "You taught me to remain calm", as Athena had exemplified "calm" throughout the experience. I've learned a lot from Athena over the years. I am so grateful for our very precious friendship!

# Goodbyes

*Don't count the days, make the days count.*

—Muhammad Ali

**ANOTHER THING THAT** my beloved friend, Athena, taught me was how to say goodbye without too much heartbreak. She always kept her goodbyes extremely short and very sweet. I learned from her to say, "Goodbye", and leave as quickly as possible.

Over the years, every time we said adieu, neither of us knew when we'd see each other again...particularly during my dark years of being married to Horace Jones. He was jealous of anyone I loved and with whom I was close. I tried to see Athena whenever I could, but my life with Jones was unpredictable and spending time with her was both sporadic and perilous.

The most significant goodbye that Athena and I shared was when she and her husband, Dennis, were about to emigrate from South Africa to Europe. They had booked to leave the evening of my mother's funeral. Athena walked up to me and said, "Fof"—she always called me "Fof", which is short for "Photinee", my paternal grandmother's nickname and after whom I was named—"Fof, I need to go now". And then she gave me a hug and a kiss on each cheek and was gone. Parting is much better that way.

I've taken this lesson to heart. At every painful parting that I've ever experienced, and particularly with family members who live in other countries, I have kept my goodbyes short, sweet, and speedy.

# Why Did I Stay?

*Here's to matrimony, the high sea for which no compass has yet been invented!*

—Heinrich Heine

**MANY, MANY PEOPLE** have asked me why I stayed in a verbally and physically abusive marriage to Horace Jones for sixteen years.

A close friend of mine remarked, "Tina, you are not a walk in the park. You are very strict in terms of your values. You've stood up against tyrants in the workplace. You're a strong, strong woman and you're a brave woman. Why the hell did you stay in that marriage for sixteen years when it was abusive"?

Or, a question from a young lady, who didn't know me well but who'd done some research on me, "I've heard through the grapevine that you had an abusive marriage. Can you tell us more and can you tell us why you stayed in an abusive marriage"?

Well, the long and short of it is that, first and foremost, I believe in forgiveness. Secondly, I believe that love changes everything. And thirdly, one of my biggest challenges, namely, that I never put myself first and never will put myself first. These three reasons were the ones that impelled me to stay, and made me determined to break Horace Jones's cycle of abuse. After all, I did love the man. My reasons are not unique, but typical of women who are abused, and there has been a lot of research done on these reasons.

### My Biggest Mistake

My biggest mistake, however, was that I hid the fact that I was being physically abused. My closest friends and family knew of the verbal abuse (some had witnessed it), but nobody, other than my brother and his wife, knew of the physical abuse. And the only reason that they knew was because, after one episode, I had escaped to their home and it was plain to see that I had been beaten. Horace Jones had pulled a chunk of my hair out, leaving a big bald patch. My sister-in-law had very gently and lovingly braided my hair to hide the bald patch, so that it wouldn't alarm my parents when we visited them the next day. Nobody else knew about Horace Jones's violence until I had finally left him for good.

In our sixteen years of marriage, the physical abuse happened six or seven times, but the verbal abuse was a regular phenomenon. One can heal from physical beating, but verbal violence pierces the heart and does irreparable damage. Having learnt by inverse, my message to women is, "Never stay in an abusive relationship. If abuse occurs even *once*, that's one time too many. I repeat, if you are ever abused verbally or physically, leave immediately".

### A Real Shocker

Horace Jones's first verbal lashing took place the night before we married. My only excuse for pardoning him is that I was very young, twenty-three years old, and I was in love.

All the arrangements for the wedding were in place and, after he lashed out at me, I was in shock.

So often in life, we hold onto what we want to be the reality, but isn't. We filter out the negative. So, I rationalised Horace's behavior by reassuring myself that he had spoken to me in such an offensive manner because he was nervous about the wedding and was under a lot of stress at work. I let it go, which I should not have done. I should have listened to my gut and immediately called off the wedding.

### A SELF-PROCLAIMED ASS

The first time Horace Jones beat me, I was devastated and I left him, as I did every time he beat me thereafter. He always beat me when I was alone, never when Eric was home with me. Eric spent many weekends at my parents' home or with his sporting friends. Each time he beat me, I'd leave, certain that I'd never return to him. But every single time I left, he came to me begging for forgiveness.

Ten days was the longest period of silence between us, but usually after about a week, Horace Jones would approach my dad and tell him how remorseful he was and that he didn't deserve me. On three of these occasions, he lamented to my father that he was a "dirty dog". My dad relayed to me that Horace had told him, "Tina is the best thing that ever happened to me. She's a remarkable wife and a good woman. I'm an ass, Axios! I don't deserve Tina. I'm going to get professional help". Of course, my dad thought we had argued. He never knew I'd been beaten.

On occasion, Jones even told his children, with whom I had grown very close, that he was going for therapy and that he should not have behaved the way he did. Horace Jones was authentic. He was truly very, very sorry. I believe that he was an obsessive compulsive and that the cycle of abuse, with which he had grown up, was something that he could not escape without therapy. But, sadly, he never went for therapy. I was able to survive. I hated the whole thing, but I loved him and I forgave him each time.

And there were good times. In fact, there were wonderful times. He was extremely kind to me in between the bouts of verbal and physical abuse and unwaveringly loving to my family. And so I stayed.

### PENDULUM, PARADOX AND POISON

Horace Jones swung like a pendulum from being kind, generous and loving to becoming an utter terror, an absolute Jekyll and Hyde. And dear Jimmy, our driver! Jimmy was an elderly Ndebele man, and the Ndebele are extremely gracious people. Jimmy had worked for Horace Jones for over twenty years when I came on the scene. He was very loyal, but Jones spared no one his poisonous tongue. Oh, how he spewed venom with that tongue, so unbelievably damaging and wicked! And Jimmy often received the brunt of it.

After one such skewering outburst aimed at Jimmy, Jimmy was visibly heartbroken. Like me and like everyone else who was punished by that tongue, Jimmy hadn't done anything wrong. One Friday afternoon as we were driving to the bank to do Jones's payroll, Jimmy just shook his head—he was a wise, old man—and he said to me, "When the boss is good, he is very, very good, and when he is bad, he is horrid", quoting a children's verse someone had shared with him along the line.

And so, whether it was me, his workers, or his family members—his own children had received this abuse, as well—there was never grounding for the abuse. There never was a reason. The six or seven times that I was beaten were the result of me standing up for others. It never was for anything I had done.

As I said previously, I loved the man and I would not have done anything to upset him. I learnt to read him very, very quickly. I am perceptive. I am an empath. And so I knew exactly what to do and what not to do. But...when I see other people being harmed, I cannot and will not hold myself back. And, so, every occasion of abuse was in retaliation of me protecting someone else.

## DEFENDER OF THE DEFENSELESS

One of the worst beatings I received was punishment for protecting Horace's own grandson. We were at home and Reggie and Eric were swimming. Horace arrived home from work and started to ridicule and mock the youngster for being overweight. He then began to insult Reggie's mother who, at the time, was Horace's daughter-in-law. This dear child was only one year younger than my own son and I loved him. I'd known him since he was a toddler. I went crazy in his defense. And...I paid the price.

I deeply considered all that I'd read about abuse; that it's a cycle and that, when children are subjected to it, they emulate it. I knew that Horace had been abused by his older brother, who had beaten him repeatedly. I knew that there had been a lot of verbal abuse in his family. And I knew that he had abused his first wife. And, so, I took it upon myself, to break the cycle, if not for myself, for his children and grandchildren. And that is why I stayed in my marriage to Horace Jones for sixteen years.

Ultimately, I left Jones because he started to get jealous of my beloved son, Eric, as he grew into manhood. Yes, that is when I had the strength to leave my husband. As for myself, well, people can do virtually anything to me and I rebound. But go near someone I love, and I'll kill you.

# Mensch

*What do we live for if it is not to make life less difficult for each other?*

—Mary Ann Evans, aka George Eliot

**I WAS BORN** and grew up in Elangeni in the old Transvaal, now called Gauteng, South Africa. The suburb in which I lived, Lennox, had a huge Jewish population. On Jewish holidays, there was hardly anyone at school. In fact, sometimes we used to have the day off because there were so many Jewish children in our class, that it didn't warrant the rest of the children being there.

And, so, a lot of my early childhood, my culture, my outlook, and my vocabulary, included some Jewish words. I knew the word *mensch,* and I thought I knew what it meant. But I had not met a real *mensch* until I met Caryn Green in New York, many years later.

Caryn is extraordinary. She extends herself to be a true friend. If she were older and larger than me (she's tiny), I could equate her with a mother figure. Caryn does for me what a mother would do for a child. She is only a phone call away, if I need her. Most of my friends are lifelong friends and it was delightful to have such a sincere new friend so soon after coming to New York in 2011.

It was from the very beginning that she extended this hand of *philotimo,* which is a Greek word that means "the love of human beings". The word *philanthropy and philotimo* are derived from the same root word, *philo* or *friend. Philotimo* goes deeper, though. It means to have honor and integrity. It means to be open and transparent. It means to care. And my definition of *care* is *love-in-action.* And that is Caryn. Caryn is *love-in-action.* She has guided me in many ways, always expressing great care and tenderness. Not only did she embrace me with her philotimo, she extended it to my son and his lovely fiancé too. Only a true *mensch* has *philotimo.*

# Grand Finale

*We must open the doors and we must see to it they remain open, so that others can pass through.*

—Rosemary Brown

**WHEN I MET** Caryn in 2011, she and her business partner, Debbie, were organising a full day at the United Nations for a hundred and ninety-two girls to fill the UN's one hundred and ninety-two seats. The day was the culmination of the last day of the Year of the Child. Secretary General Ban Ki Moon had mandated Caryn and Debbie to plan the event. They had very skillfully crafted an agenda for the day. And they had asked me to facilitate a round-table discussion with some of the girls, who were tasked with changing the world.

These were young women, the ages of whom ranged from eleven to twenty-two. Some of the projects that they came up with were absolutely mind-blowing. It's amazing what can be done when young people are given freedom to innovate. When they haven't been clipped by the real world, and haven't had their big ideas truncated by people who put them in boxes and by naysayers who say, "You can't do this.

You can't do that. That's impossible". It was green fields for these girls. They were thinking big and came up with phenomenal projects.

Caryn had run the agenda by me. What was missing was a grand finale, and I wasn't shy to say so. They asked me if I had any ideas.

"I absolutely do", I said.

I introduced Caryn to my friend, Matilda, from South Africa, who runs an extraordinary not–for-profit organization that educates underprivileged children and orphans of AIDS at the tertiary level. Matilda had a superstar alumna of her program, Miriam, who became head of a household when both her parents died of AIDS. Miriam had graduated and was in the workplace, and she was a very competent public speaker. We managed to fly her from South Africa to New York to address the young girls at the UN at the end of the day's events.

Miriam simply told her story. It was the quintessential grand finale. There wasn't a dry eye in the house. Miriam spoke exceedingly well...nothing soppy, no dramatics, but just the reality and from the heart.

She was superb. It was a phenomenal ending to a phenomenal day. I salute Caryn, who worked tirelessly to make the event meaningful and impactful for the young women. It certainly was memorable and a huge privilege for me to be involved.

# Doing What It Takes

*There is no royal, flower-strewn path to success. And if there is, I have not found it. For if I have accomplished anything in life, it is because I have been willing to work hard.*

—C.J. Walker

**IN 1988, I** owned a bakery in a suburban Shopping Center in Iliwa. The name of my business was *The Delicious Oven*. I had five qualified bakers, but things got tough when my head baker, Koeni, had a heart attack one week before Christmas.

Koeni was the only person who knew my pie recipes and how to make them—meat pies and chicken pies, cheese pies and spinach pies—and I had massive orders to fill. We usually turned out seven-hundred-and-fifty pies a day. We cooked the meat for the meat pies in enormous ten-kilogram pots. Knowing that these orders must go out and that none of the other bakers could make these pies, I went in at 3 a.m. each day that week to cook the meat, so that when my bakers arrived at 5 a.m., the filling for the pies was ready.

On the third morning of this 3 a.m. ritual, I was stirring

the meat in the big pots with my arms raised high to be able to reach the spoon into the mixture, when I had a spasm. The muscles contracted and my shoulders and arms froze. The pain was indescribable. I managed to turn the stove off and shuffle over to my desk to phone my mother. While choking back tears, I said "I don't know what to do. I can't move". My mother advised me to wait until someone showed up at the bakery and ask them to take me to the doctor. She offered to come help me, but she lived at least an hour's drive away and I knew that, by the time she got ready, she wouldn't arrive for at least an hour-and-a-half.

Fortunately, the pharmacist who owned the pharmacy opposite *The Delicious Oven* used to arrive very early in the morning. I stood at the window watching for him. When he arrived, I went outside and screamed for him. He came over to me and said, "You need to have an injection. You need immediate relaxation of those muscles". He helped me lock up and put a note on the door to let the bakers know to wait for my return. The pharmacist then took me to the nearby Iliwa Hospital where I was given several injections and anti-inflammatories. Within an hour, I was able to put my arms down, although the pain was still severe. We had a lot to accomplish that day and the pharmacist kindly took me back to the bakery. By that stage, my staff had arrived and I was able to instruct them how to make the pies, even though I was still immobilized. Thank goodness my mother arrived soon thereafter!

Filling our orders that day was not an option. It was mandatory. And I rose to the occasion. After all, when the going gets tough...

# The Proverbial Duck

*Success is not the key to happiness. Happiness is the key to success. If you love what you are doing, you will be successful.*

—Albert Schweitzer

**PEOPLE OFTEN RESPOND** to a challenging task or situation with, "I'll do my best", but in my book, that's not enough. I want people to do *whatever it takes* to successfully complete the job...to go *beyond* one's best. I've always had to do whatever it takes...to go the extra mile and, as one of my mentors said, "It's a very lonely mile on that road with no traffic on it".

For example, when I was interviewed for a job at the Oasis Hotel and was asked if I were proficient on the computer. I had never touched a computer before and I knew that would be a deal breaker. So, praying that God would forgive me for lying, I answered, "Yes". I got the job and was to begin working three days later. I sold some of my jewelry to be able to pay for a crash course in basic computing skills over the weekend. By the Monday morning, my first day of work, I had the basic knowledge I needed.

## The Spreadsheet Blues

The following week, as a brand new employee, I was handed a hard copy of the contact details of almost a thousand members of the Iliwa Association. My boss asked me to transfer all the members onto an Excel spreadsheet by the end of the month. One month to capture all those members with their details, and I had had only a few hours of training in Excel during my elementary computer course!

After one week of entering the data, I was in excruciating pain and eventually I couldn't move. I called Eric, who was at university at the time, to ask him to go to the pharmacy to get me some muscle relaxants and a special cushion for hemorrhoids and then bring them to my office. I had spent so many hours sitting at my computer that I had developed hemorrhoids and I could not sit any longer. My rear end was in agony, and my shoulders and arms were so stiff that I could hardly move. I waited for Eric to arrive with relief.

After work, I put my special donut-shaped cushion on my car seat, slowly lowered myself into the car, and made it home. And that is how I learnt to use the computer, no one the wiser. Eventually, I did become proficient.


## Meteoric Rise?

People seem to think that success is easy…that life is easy…and this irritates me. They think you go to bed and wake up the next day successful! I'll never forget how flustered I got when a friend commented on my "meteoric rise", referring to my business success.

I just shook my head and said, "You have no idea of the hard work that got me where I am…how many hours I sat writing up processes, policies and procedures and traveling the world …how meticulously I monitored everything… and the huge personal sacrifices I made".

People don't understand that, when things are going smoothly, it's often because one has mastered what one's work is. They don't realise that it's like the proverbial duck that glides gracefully on top of the water but, underneath, it is pedaling like hell.

My message to young people who think they can graduate, find a great job, and start earning executive salaries right away:

You have to do your time. You must go beyond "doing your best" and show that you can do *whatever it takes*.

# Becoming CEO

*One can never consent to creep when one feels an impulse to soar.*

—Helen Keller

**I MET ANGELA** Smith on a chilly June morning in 2003. She was the Chairman of the *Iliwa Chapter of the United Business Women* a chapter of the National UBW. Angela had come to the Oasis Hotel, where I was working, to check the venue for her annual *Business Award Gala Dinner*. As was usually the case, when someone of importance arrived at the Oasis Hotel, I was called upon to present the hotel and conference grounds. The minute I shook her hand, I knew that I would know Angela for the rest of my life.

Angela is a beautiful woman. Tall with exquisite blue eyes, a lovely countenance and a strong handshake, she has presence and elegance. She is articulate and well-spoken. We bonded instantly over breakfast. Afterwards, I gave her the grand tour of the grounds. As we went along, laughing and joking, Angela shared more about the UBW. I had not heard of the organisation and was intrigued.

In 2001, immediately after my training in Perth at the headquarters of the Australian teaching franchise I owned, I was told to find a woman's business organisation when I returned home and to join it. The Internet was not yet being fully searched as it is now, so all I could find were sector-specific organisations that didn't suit my business model. And, so, I was pleasantly surprised during this first encounter with Angela to learn about the UBW. Angela shared with me how great it was to be able to participate in and organise workshops and other events, all of which were educational and geared toward business. It was fascinating. I asked Angela to add me to the UBW's database and promised to attend some of their functions.

## A DREAM COME TRUE

One week later, I received my first email from the UBW. It was an appeal, sent out to the ten thousand members of the UBW, asking for a referral of a woman who could successfully run the Iliwa branch. The coordinator, Cheryl, had just resigned with one month's notice, so the search for her replacement had begun immediately. I took this news in and thought, "That's the type of job I'd like to have".

Without any further ado, I emailed Angela and told her that I wanted to apply for the job. Angela responded to my email, saying that I was overqualified for the job and that the UBW was a not-for-profit and didn't pay well. She also mentioned that she thought that the CEO, who had been interviewing all week, had already found someone to take Cheryl's place.

I telephoned Angela immediately and said, "Angela, I'm serious. I really want this job. It seems as though it's just made for me. I have all the skills listed, and it has been a dream of mine to empower women. I just know that I'd fit in. And I'd love to work for you". Angela laughed and repeated that I was overqualified and that the UBW doesn't pay well.

I said, "Angela, this is a conscious decision I'm making. My son is working now and he is earning well. I no longer need to work as a means to an end, but rather choose to work with a purpose". She promised me that she would contact the CEO, and ask her how far she was with the interviewing process.

A week later, I received a phone call from Angela, who said, "I have good news for you. The CEO said she will meet with you. But, managing expectations, when she saw your CV, she didn't think that you'd want to work for so little remuneration". Well, I met with the CEO, an incredible strategist and a great inspiration. And it wasn't an interview, but a fabulous conversation.

"Look, I really want to do this. I'm ready for it", I said.

At that stage, I had been working for twenty-five years and strongly felt that it was time to do something that I loved and give back by sharing my experiences with women, and to learn from the other women, as well.

I got the job and was overjoyed. To this day, I am deeply grateful to have worked with Angela, a leader and a motivator who could evoke the best from me.

## TRAILBLAZING

Angela and I did some incredible things together—events, workshops and fundraisers, among other things, that raised the profile of the entire organisation. These were Angela's ideas that I was implementing, but she allowed me to take initiative. She allowed me to do things differently. She allowed me to try and experiment with things. I loved it. I blossomed. I had a boss who believed in me. Angela was a boss who enabled me to use my talents. I put processes and procedures in place. I changed the way certain things had been done and made them more efficient and easier. I thoroughly enjoyed the events. I was learning so much! I was reaching out to incredible people and meeting people who, previously, I could only dream of meeting. And all along, Angela allowed me to grow. Her example was extraordinary. She is such a lady. She is so professional and polished. I watched and learned.

## How to Fire a Client

Angela even taught me how to fire a client. There was a member of the UBW who complained about literally everything we did. We had just changed the venue for our monthly meetings and this member arrived flustered and squawking loudly. She walked up to Angela to greet her, complaining loudly for all to hear. I don't know how she did it, but Angela was unwaveringly charming and warm throughout the exchange.

After listening for a second or two, she shook the woman's hand and said, "I've heard you. Perhaps this organisation is not for you".

The woman was shocked and, backpedaling, said, "No, no, no! I want to be here. I love the organisation"!

"Please, then, accept what is. Give us your suggestions, but this is neither the time nor the place to complain and moan", replied Angela.

Angela was firm and bold. Wow, what a valuable lesson. It was from this experience that I later developed my workshop, "How to Fire a Client". I learnt so much from that incident. I gained so much from Angela's strength and her ability to stand up and interrupt, if things weren't going correctly… to stand up and be a master of ceremonies of note…to stand up and comment on a speaker…and to take questions and answers in such a purely sophisticated and graceful way.

## Joyful Work

I worked long hours because I loved the work. I relished every day. I couldn't wait to get up in the morning and check my emails to see what happened overnight. What an incredible four months!

And why only four months? With all that we were achieving and all the rave reviews from the sponsors, the UBW's head office and CEO took notice. The CEO knew that Angela was incredible, no matter which coordinator she had. She also knew that I was able to be extremely dedicated…that I could be strong and pass along what I had established in the way of processes and procedures…and that I could certainly influence the other coordinators of the other chapters. Thus, the CEO told Angela that she wanted me to take over the role of National Coordinator at the head office and to roll out the systems I had put in place for the Iliwa chapter to all of South Africa.

It was with great sadness that Angela and I parted ways as employer-employee, but it wasn't a full parting. Angela sat on the UBW Council, the board of the UBW, so I would still see her often, but I wouldn't be working directly with her. It is for this reason alone that my promotion to National Coordinator was bittersweet. A year later, when I applied for the CEO position, Angela was part of the committee that interviewed me initially. The second and third rounds of interviews were performed without Angela present. But I had learnt enough from her by that time and became the CEO of UBW. Ultimately, I answered to the Council and, hence, to Angela once again.

Angela has remained a great confidant and a precious friend throughout the years. I wish that I could see her frequently for a dose of her contagious goodness, the spark that Angela possesses, and for the fun loving person that she is. Angela extended a hand and helped me up, and I'll never forget it. I am very grateful to her for stretching me and enabling me to reach my potential.

# XX

*The bad news is time flies. The good news is you're the pilot.*

—Michael Althsuler

**MEN PERPLEX ME.**

I haven't dated many men. Out of the few men I dated, I married two. The first, my childhood sweetheart Jim, who is the father of my beloved son; and the second, Horace, two years after I divorced Jim.

### X Number 1

I met Jim when I was fourteen years old. I was brought up strictly, so my brother was required to chaperone us on all our dates. We even had a chaperone throughout our one-year engagement. All in all, our courtship was quintessentially Greek. We married in 1978, one day after my nineteenth birthday.

Within a week of being married, Jim changed. I am a traditionalist and believe that the man is head of the marriage. Therefore, I refused to tell him what to do and what not to do. Thus, when he tasted this newfound freedom, something he hadn't had growing up with in a home even stricter than mine, he went off the rails. He started to smoke, which I abhor, and he attended a lot of office parties with its correlative consumption of alcohol…with infidelity soon to follow.

Jim knew that cigarette smoke repelled me, but he didn't care. I refused to let him come close to me because of the stench, but it made no difference, and his philandering increased. The irony is that, when I finally divorced him, he had the nerve to tell people that I was frigid. Yes, I didn't want him near me because he stank and I couldn't tolerate the smoking, let alone that I was painfully aware of his indiscretions, but frigid? No.

I threw Jim out of my townhouse, a home that my father had secured for me, on Jim's birthday, the tenth of January. The date was significant in another way. "10 January 1960" is engraved on my Christening Cross as the day I was baptised.

I had invited Jim's entire family over to celebrate his birthday. Only I was aware that, before his family arrived, Jim had blatantly telephoned one of his mistresses right in front of me to tell her that he'd be over to visit her as soon as his party had concluded.

Our son Eric was ten months old at the time and, as we were having our tea and cake, he choked on a biscuit. Everybody panicked, yelling and cursing at me for giving Eric the biscuit against the advice of my father-in-law. Of course, Eric was fine. He had had biscuits every day for the past week without any episodes. I was sick and tired of people jumping to conclusions and not knowing what I was going through with Jim. Without fanfare, I asked everyone, including Jim, to leave. A month later, I divorced him.

## X Number 2

Two years later, and by chance, I met Horace Jones.

My lifelong friend, Gladys, had gone on a blind date with

Horace Jones's best friend, Joe. And she had told Joe that she could cook Greek pastitsio, a kind of Greek lasagna. Gladys invited Joe over for dinner and then asked me if I would prepare the pastitsio and slip it to her at the last minute before her date arrived.

I prepared the pastitsio and took it over. With my hands full, I kicked open the bottom half of the door and said, "Die kos is op die tafel", which is Afrikaans for "The food is on the table". When I walked in, there were two men sitting in Gladys's lounge. Evidently, Joe and his friend Horace had gambled at the racetrack and lost their money that afternoon. Joe didn't want to drive Horace all the way back to Iliwa before having dinner with Gladys, so he had insisted that Horace come along on his date. It was only long after the fact that I learnt of this.

Both men were around my father's age and so I thought nothing of it when Gladys invited me to join them for dinner. I needed company. I was vulnerable. Eric was spending the weekend with his grandparents, Jim's mom and dad, and it was going to be the first time that I had been away from my son for an entire weekend. Jim's parents adored Eric and I knew that he would be well looked after, but mine was the innate uneasiness of a young mother being parted from her child. To add to my vulnerability, my parents were away at the coast. My decision to stay was an easy one. I wanted company and I knew that the pastitsio was delicious, because I had made it.

Horace Jones was extremely handsome and charming, not to mention that he was the best dressed man I've yet to lay eyes on. And he was athletic, having been a soccer player all his life. Horace began to flirt with me. When he asked for my telephone number at the end of the evening, I didn't want to give it to him. Rather, I told him to give me his phone number and that I'd call him.

---

A couple of days later, Gladys told me that Joe had phoned her many times on behalf of his friend to ask for my telephone number. As I considered calling Horace Jones, I finally asked myself, "What have I got to lose? I enjoyed his company. He has a good sense of humour, and he is extremely handsome. Well, why not"? At the fresh age of twenty-three, I was too young to make a sound judgment. I hadn't dated at all after divorcing Jim, but was focused on raising Eric and studying for my degree. Life had been really boring.

Three months later, on the twenty-fourth of November, 1983, I married the man. I knew the night before our wedding that I should not marry him, but went ahead with it anyway. Horace had swept me off my feet. Little did I know that he would also knock me off my feet…more than once.

In his insane obsessive compulsiveness, Horace Jones believed that I was the most exquisite woman walking the planet and that every man wanted me. If I greeted an old friend, a shopkeeper, or a relative, he immediately accused me of having an affair. The situation was impossible. To survive, I learned never to look in the direction of any man. I snubbed and, most likely, offended men I had known my entire life and with whom there had never been even a tinge of romance.

Between Jim and Horace, I couldn't win. The young Jim was telling the world that I was frigid and the old man thought I was 'the happy hooker'. Both exes were completely different ages, from different cultures, and in different professions, but both were passing judgment on the same woman due to their own inadequacies. How wrong they both were.

# Forgiveness

*The weak can never forgive.*
*Forgiveness is the attribute of the strong.*

—Gandhi

**MANY YEARS AGO,** I forgave both my exes.

Jim was easier to forgive than was Horace Jones, and I forgave him very quickly after we divorced. Firstly, Jim and I never argued. We were good friends. Unfortunately, it takes more to be happily married that being just good friends. Jim had always been honest with me about his affairs, which was a type of emotional torture in itself, and certainly not the right thing to do. Telling me about his flings was "scapegoating". Instead of carrying the guilt himself, he told me what he had been up to and let me feel lousy. Scapegoating is a dreadful tactic and Jim was very good at it.

He was often remorseful and, during his more penitent moments, explained that he really did love me. At one point, Jim got his act together, quit smoking and was once again the man with whom I had fallen in love. It was during this happy time that Jim gave me the greatest gift, the most profound blessing of all, my son. But Jim quickly returned to his old ways and our marital happiness was irrevocably shattered.

We married much too young. Our upbringings had been too sheltered and, while this was all right for me, it harmed Jim and kept him from developing fully as a young man.

## A TOUGHER NUT TO CRACK

Forgiving Jones was a little harder. I left him in 1999 and, after thirteen grueling months, the divorce was final. I battled with myself over forgiving him. I knew that, as a Christian, I needed to forgive, but it was difficult. This man had stolen my youth, my health, and everything I owned. When I married him and sold my townhouse, I gave him the money. And when I left him, I left with nothing. However, I knew harboring such resentment would harm me.

In 2005, I addressed a group of young women at a meeting. One of them had done her homework on the CEO of the UBW. She asked me about my two marriages and if I had been able to forgive my ex-husbands. Good question! At that precise moment, I decided to forgive Jones. The event was witnessed by just over one hundred young women. Jones remained unaware.

Nine years later, in 2014, I was living in New York and still in communication with Horace's nephews, Bruce and Kevin, both of whom are wonderful men. Kevin had reached out to me several times to say, "You know, Uncle Horace asks about you". Each time, I'd divert the conversation by asking about Kevin's lovely family and his business.

But in August 2014, Kevin sent me a message via Facebook. "I'd like to speak to you. Can you give me your US telephone number"? he asked.

I sent him my number and he called me. Kevin said, "Uncle Horace really wants to speak to you. Give him a ring.

It's his birthday tomorrow". Of course, I knew it was Horace Jones's birthday. Kevin is a superb salesman, as well as an eloquent man, and he said all the right things. We ended our conversation with him giving me Horace's phone number.

I didn't think anything more of it.

But that night, as I prayed before I went to sleep, I felt a powerful conviction that I had to phone Horace because, perhaps, what he wanted was to hear me say, "I forgive you". I hadn't spoken a word to him in fourteen years!

I reached out for guidance. "Dear Lord, what do I say? What do I do"?

I fell asleep and, when I awoke the next morning, I knew had to call him.

The day started off busy and I forgot about calling Horace. I had a meeting coming up and, as I checked the time, I remembered to call. I had only minutes before it would be too late in Iliwa, South Africa to wish him a happy birthday. Without any hesitation, I dialed the number. The minute Horace answered, it was a though no time had lapsed. He answered in the same way as he always had...simple and abrupt.

"Jones"!

"Hello, Horace Jones", I said. "Happy birthday". He recognized my voice.

"Hello, my sweetheart! How are you"? Was his jubilant response.

This was surreal because our divorce had been so bitter. It was amazing to hear his happy voice. Straightaway, he asked me all sorts of questions about my family, my brother, my sister, my son, and then he asked, "Did you ever remarry"?

"No", I said, even though I knew that Horace was already aware of this.

He said, "I never remarried either." He went on, "I'm very well and I go to church every Wednesday morning". From the ensuing silence, I knew that I had done the right thing to call.

I replied, "That's wonderful. I am so glad for you. God is great".

A long pause followed.

It was done.

Then he spoke about all sorts of other things, including how he goes for walks every day.

"You know, my sweetheart, I am eighty-two today", he said.

He made me promise that I would phone again and I said I would, but I haven't. It's not necessary. I knew that that call was the important one.

"You've made my day. You've made my week. And you've made my year. Thank you, thank you, thank you, my sweetheart"!

I had forgiven him and he felt it. I didn't have to say the words.

He knew.

It felt good.

# Ray Of Sunshine

*Every time you smile at someone, it is an action of love, a gift to that person, a beautiful thing.*

—Mother Teresa

**IN NOVEMBER 2013,** I headed to Santiago, Chile to attend an international conference and award ceremony. I was attending as Global Director of a company I worked for at the time. My aim was to initiate a relationship with the International organisation and cultivate a partnership. Previously, this international organization had only partnered with chambers of commerce. The awards they bestow at their annual conference are some of the most prestigious awards, worldwide, that a woman entrepreneur can receive. Irene Ping happened to be an honoree that year and she was from New York.

## LAUGHTER

This conference, as do most conferences, included tedious bus trips. During one of these bus trips, I heard contagious laughter coming from the back of the bus. Everyone turned around to see who was laughing, but the laughter stopped and we couldn't find the instigator. However, when I boarded the bus, I had noticed an extremely well-dressed woman who stood out from the others. She wore a broad smile on her face and wasn't wearing the traditional skirt and jacket business suit attire that many women wear to conferences. She was different. I suspected that it was she who initiated the joviality.

The next day, when the honorees were on stage, I was stunned to hear one of the honorees, Irene, who is Asian, speak to the conference goers in fluent Spanish. I made a mental note to connect with Irene because, by that stage, I had realised that the contagious laughter on the bus had been hers. Oh, how I love happy and positive people!

As it goes with such events though, the packed agenda provided very little free time, and whatever free time we did have overflowed with people connecting and catching up with one another. I only managed to speak a few words with Irene the evening we were invited to the ambassador's home. I was talking with her sister and her niece and Irene had come over for a photograph with us.

### GUIDED BY FEELING

The conference concluded with the gala dinner and awards evening. I entered the large ballroom and decided not to sit in my allocated seat up front. I wanted to be near the exit so that I could escape if the proceedings ran late. Rather, I walked around to see where I *felt* good. I seriously don't always remember people's faces and I seldom remember their names, but I always remember how people make me feel. As I zigzagged through the tables, I felt warmth and goodness coming from a sparsely occupied table of Asian women.

"Do you mind if I take a seat"? I asked.

An extraordinarily stylish woman, whom I later found out, was Irene's mother, smiled and gestured for me to sit down.

She didn't speak much English, but we understood each other perfectly through gestures and facial expressions. I felt welcomed and very comfortable. Shortly thereafter, Irene's sister arrived and sat down at my other side. One of their friends joined us too. I soon realised that Irene's mother could understand quite a bit of English, and we had a lovely conversation with the help of the others at the table who spoke good English. What a pleasant evening I had chatting with Irene's mom! Although Irene had to sit at the front with the other honorees, I was happily ensconced in her family.

## A MEETING OF MINDS

Unbeknown to me, Irene had shared her plans to expand her business beyond the United States with her many connections at the conference. Irene later told me that everyone with whom she had shared her expansion plans had replied, "Oh, in that case, you need to speak to Tina Thomson". At that stage, she didn't know who I was.

Naturally, when I returned to New York, I sent an email to each of the honorees to congratulate them and, also, to pitch the organisation I worked for to them. As the honorees of this award, they had the exact profile of the entrepreneurs we wanted for our organisation. To my delight, I received a wonderful email from Irene in reply, inviting me to visit her at her New Jersey office. She proposed some dates with the promise to send her driver to collect and return me to New York City. I agreed to a meeting on the eighteenth of December and thought nothing more of it, other than I was looking forward to meeting this wonderful, joyous individual face-to-face.

## EXIT STAGE LEFT

I had already planned my exit from the company I worked for before I met with Irene. Although I loved my work, it had been nearly six years of nonstop traveling, averaging fourteen-hour work days, at least six days a week. No matter how much I had accomplished, the work was never done. We were building the organisation and I gave it my all. I was extremely fatigued and realised that I had no life outside of work. I wanted to settle down in the U.S., close to my son. I also wanted a chance at having a relationship, which was impossible with the way I traveled. Add to this, the betrayal and salary slashing by the Founder and I was ready to leave.

And, so, I exited the company I had nurtured on the thirteenth of December, five days before I was to meet with Irene Ping. I completed the paperwork which finalized my exit from that company on the morning of the eighteenth, the day I was meeting with Irene. Admittedly, I was quite hesitant as to whether or not I should go because I thought that Irene would want to talk about becoming a member of my former company, an organisation of which I was now no longer a part.

I decided to listen to my intuition, which kept saying, "Go, just go. You need to make friends in New York. Irene is a delightful individual and, quite frankly, you don't have anything to do now that you are not working". I showered, dressed, and went into Manhattan to see my son and his fiancé Ariel, who lived close to where Irene's driver, Josh, was to meet me.

## COMPLETELY BLOWN AWAY

What an incredible experience! Only Irene Ping could have orchestrated something so wonderful. From the minute I met her driver, Josh, and climbed into Irene's company car, I felt the world embrace me. Not only was there beautiful music playing in the car, there was water and snacks on hand. I wondered just how far New Jersey was from Manhattan, as I had never been. I figured that New Jersey must be quite a distance away, if food and drink were provided. Well, it wasn't far at all. The water and snacks were thoughtful gestures of Irene's hospitality. Forty minutes later, we arrived at Irene's company.

When I walked into the building, I was struck instantly by the vibrant colours and magnificent products. I felt as if I had fallen down a hole into a fabulous party in Wonderland. Nothing could have prepared me for this. I knew that Irene's company was a leader in the party, gifting, educational, and stationery supplies industries, but I was completely unprepared for the exquisite twenty-thousand-square-foot showroom.

The pièce de résistance was a large television screen displaying a photograph of Irene's entire team smiling and waving with the words, "Welcome, Tina Thomson" on it. I was speechless.

The young man who greeted me gave me an overview of the company, after which his colleague gave me a tour of the premises. I was then shown to the boardroom. I heard Irene approach before I saw her. I heard her laughter…the authentic joy in her voice. The door opened and there she was.

Our conversation was primarily about membership in my former company. I sold her on the idea and told her that I'd introduce her to the women who could complete her membership, but she wanted me to handle it. That's when I told her that I had exited the company. The minute I told Irene that I was unemployed she asked me what I was going to do next. I told her that I hadn't decided yet and was going to take a break to rest, but that, in January, I would begin the search for a job. She looked down at her wristwatch and said, "I have to go into a meeting, but are you able to wait an hour and then have dinner with me"?

I said, "Yes".

## DINNER

Throughout our conversation over dinner, I marveled at the pace at which Irene's brilliant mind ticked forward, but also at the extremely relevant questions she was asking. From that meeting, I knew that Irene was a gifted businesswoman with a bright and inquiring mind. Her warmth and generous spirit were remarkable.

Irene is intriguing. She is a lifelong learner. When she shared with me that she was investigating taking a business course through a European business school, I was surprised because Irene already had an MBA. When I asked her why, she said, "My MBA was a while ago and I studied in New York. I want to take a course outside of the U.S. and get up to date with trends and the way business has changed globally". Remarkable. We talked about all sorts of other things, too. I left Irene, who was about to leave for Asia to visit her parents over the Christmas holidays, and Josh drove me home.

## A GLORIOUS OPPORTUNITY

In January, we picked up our conversation. Irene wanted me to work for her company. By the time she made me the offer, I was already entertaining several others, but hadn't decided on any of them. Fortunately, my dear friend, Athena, was visiting me for a week and, as it was a particularly arctic winter, we were home a lot of the time and could discuss my various employment options.

Athena said to me, "Some of these offers are amazing and grand, with huge packages, but I have a really good feeling about Irene". Athena was correct. Athena is wise and always correct.

Irene is a *good* soul...someone who goes way beyond what a boss 'should' do for employees. I've witnessed her extend a helping hand to her employees on many occasions.

I've watched her take people from A to Z, equipping them with everything they need, and then give them wings to fly. Irene is a leader in every sense of the word. And I am a recipient of her kindness. There is no end to her thoughtfulness. She is one of the greatest entrepreneurial leaders I have met throughout the world. To God be the glory for my opportunity to work with such an incredible role model as Irene Ping.

# Tropical Holidays

*There is no more creative force in the world than the menopausal woman with zest.*

—Margaret Mead

**I ENTERED THAT** life-altering stage in female biology, the dreaded menopause, towards the end of 2009. And it did me in. I ran hot all the time and was certain that, at any moment, I'd spontaneously combust. By the end of 2010, the hot flashes or "tropical holidays", as I came to call them, appeared quite suddenly and dramatically and I felt as if I were on fire—and not in a good way—at least twice every hour, day and night.

The situation was delicate. When the tropical holiday descended during the day, I'd frantically strip down to my birthday suit, whenever and wherever I could. To add to my misery, a cold front would move in right before each hot flash and, shivering, I'd bundle up, only to rip it all off a few minutes later when the situation really heated up. This became routine. Both the cold spells and hot flashes got progressively worse.

## A NEW COUNTRY

In 2011, I moved to New York from South Africa. This was exciting as I was finally able to secure a Special Skills or H-1B visa to work in the US and be near my son. The relocation was fraught with drama after drama, though, and life was challenging. During the tropical storms, I radiated so much heat that the furniture upon which I was lying or sitting became hot to the touch. I'd fling open the windows in the middle of a New York winter and stand there naked, trying desperately to regulate my temperature. While I hoped that no one witnessed these episodes, cooling down took precedence over modesty.

Having moved to New York, my next step was to get a Social Security Number. I had been told that all I needed to do was to go to the Social Security office with my passport, stamped with my visa, and they'd give me a number. Easy, right? No. After standing in line for an hour-and-a-half and being addressed repeatedly as a "Non-immigrant Alien," rather than by my name, the man behind the desk called me up, looked at my passport and visa, and said, "Oh, you've only been in the country three days". And then he closed my passport and told me that I needed to return in two weeks because people with my qualifications typically didn't stay.

"You'll be gone in two weeks' time", he said.

I protested. "I need to stay. My son lives here", said I, but he insisted that I wait and return to the office in two weeks. This, in turn, delayed me from being able to open a bank account, obtain medical insurance, and other things. Months after the fact, I learned that the Social Security worker had erred and that I should have been issued my card the first time I came in.

Besides the stress of relocating countries, and the biological blizzards and tropical holidays, I ended up needing dental surgery, which cost me the equivalent of two months' salary. The whole shebang overwhelmed me and I began to experience fainting spells.

## NOT FOR THE FAINT-HEARTED

The fainting spells were quite frightening. I could feel them coming on and would lower myself to the ground beforehand, so I wouldn't fall and hurt myself. My father had once said, "If you read up, any illness that has .002% sufferers, that's Tina". The fainting spells and their accompanying dizziness were extreme symptoms of menopause that very few women experience. Finally, I sought medical help.

My precious friend Caryn, my mensch, referred me to a doctor who treated me for the dizzy spells and fainting. I begged to go on Hormone Replacement Therapy, as well. I needed to sleep. I had a demanding job and had to be fully functional all day long. The symptoms assuaged and, after three years, I was able to discontinue the treatment and land on the other side of menopause in one piece.

# Merlin...The Great!

*In learning you will teach, in teaching you will learn.*

— Phil Collins

**"TINA IS THE** grit in the oyster!" Long pause… "But she does produce pearls."

These words were spoken by a young woman who started working for me straight out of university and who, five years later was appointed as a senior executive in a multinational corporation. The embarrassing part was that she spoke these words at her wedding, which I attended.

Yes, when I see talent I cultivate it. I have extremely high standards and I do expect the same from my team. No mediocrity. No compromise. Admittedly, I do cause irritation the way the grit does in the oyster and I am relentless. But I want to stretch people to reach their full potential. And whilst my style is harsh to begin with, people always end up thanking me when they reap the benefits.

So how did I become the grit? Uncle Merlin.

Uncle Merlin taught me. He stretched me. My dad's youngest brother, Merlin Scott, (Uncle Merlin), was my very first boss.

I was only seventeen years old when I went to work for him in his business, Lennox Pharmacy. My first day on the job, my dad had made me promise to 'do more than the rest of the employees' and to 'always offer to help with extra tasks if I was not busy'. Dad was wise and well aware that I could be seen as a 'favourite' because I was the boss's niece. He needn't have bothered. Uncle Merlin knew he had to be strict with me to protect me from being bullied. He also knew that I was eager to learn and that, if I learnt good work ethics, I would be an asset to any company for which I worked in the future. I worked for Uncle Merlin for nearly four years.

### A Lifelong Mentor

Before I left South Africa, I had an opportunity to study for an MBA au gratis. I asked Uncle Merlin whether or not he thought that I should do it. He said, "What for? You've more than proved yourself, and you need to live now and not spend more time doing work-related stuff. What can an MBA teach you when you have run your own businesses and multinationals very successfully?" I took his advice and am glad I did.

The one time I didn't take his advice was in 2008, when I went to work for WCH. He had said to me, "Don't take the job," but I didn't listen. And it was disastrous.

Uncle Merlin has influenced my work style, my work ethics, and my leadership. It was he who taught me not to mix business with pleasure. He taught me it was better to keep a distance from one's employees, so that I'd have leeway to come down heavily on them, if need be, or praise them without favouritism. He taught me customer service. He taught me to be ambitious. And he certainly had a great impact on me because I admired him so much. He was the first 'married-with-kids-and-a-full-time-job-MBA-student' I had ever met. I had read about such determined people but to have one in the family was venerable indeed. Over and above running the business and studying, my Uncle was a Rotary President –twice - he also chaired the Group Study Exchange of Rotary, he was awarded the Paul Harris medal, he was a member of the prestigious Rotary Foundation…you get the picture. He was, and is, an incredible role model. But one of the truly extraordinary things about Uncle Merlin is…Aunty Sophia!

### AUNTY SOPHIA

Aunty Sophia, Uncle Merlin's wife, is gorgeous…a real traffic-stopper. As sweet as they come and always elegant and gracious, even under the duress of potential reptilian encounters, Aunty Sophia mentors me in a different way than Uncle Merlin. Always calm, and ladylike, Aunty Sophia taught me that there is a time and a place for everything.

One year at Easter, Aunty Sophia and I went to a trout farm while Uncle Merlin was away in Greece. She and I shared one of the rondavels (delightful, little guest cottages) that dotted the farm. In the bushveld, it's important to be on the lookout for scorpions and snakes. True stories abound of snakes curling up in shoes and beds, or under curtains, and it's important to stay alert.

### OPHIDIOPHOBIA

I should note here that I suffer from *ophidiophobia*, a Greek word, which means "fear of snakes". I'm also a light sleeper and, one night, I heard Aunty Sophia moving around in the adjoining alcove. What was she doing? I watched her gingerly pat down the bed.

"Aunty Sophia, are you okay?" I asked.

"Yes, My Darling. I'm sorry to disturb you. Go back to sleep," she said. But I could tell that she was distressed and she wasn't sleeping, so I couldn't either. I got out of bed and saw her standing stock still and staring at a lump underneath the covers of the bed, perplexed and petrified.

"What is it, Aunty Sophia, what is it?" I cried.

"You know My Darling," she said, "I don't really know, but when my foot touched it, it *moved.*" I felt nothing less than sheer terror and wanted to bolt out of the relative safety of our cottage and into the wild just to get away from that lump.

"Aunty Sophia, come on! It could be a snake!" I shouted.

She said, "Well, that's what I was thinking."

I wondered how she could remain so calm. "When your foot touched it, what did it feel like?" I asked.

"I don't know. It felt rather snakelike when it moved."

The lump in the middle of her bed was large. I've always been confident that I would never die of snakebite, because I'd have a heart attack and would already be dead before any snake got close enough to bite me.

But we couldn't just stand there, so I said, "Okay, here is the plan. I'm going to sweep up all the bedding, even the mattress, if I have to. You open the doors and I'm going to fling it out and then we'll quickly close the doors."

I can barely even write this story, I am so afraid of snakes. I gathered all the bedding and threw it outside. Aunty Sophia and I jumped up onto my bed, not sure why or what help that would be and then looked out the window.

### MEOW AND ADIEU

There in the tossed bedding was a cat. We both collapsed with laughter. The big lump in Aunty Sophia's bed had been a content, slumbering cat. This unassuming creature must have crawled into the bedding during the day while housekeeping was making the bed. But after the intensity and strain of the very real possibility of a snake in the bed and in the wee hours of the morning, we packed our things and drove over to the main house where my cousin Grace was staying. We waited until six-thirty when she came to the kitchen to make breakfast, bid her adieu, and took off.

## A Doting Uncle

Uncle Merlin is my dad's youngest brother by ten years and was the baby of the family. He and Aunty Sophia were engaged the year I was born, and both of them have been a constant, safe presence throughout my life. Uncle Merlin helped me with all the paperwork and difficulties I had when I lost my parents within a year of one another. They are a wonderful, second set of parents.

Jovial with a razor sharp sense of humour, Uncle Merlin is also worldly and well read. And he never misses a beat, when it comes to politics. The most remarkable thing about Uncle Merlin, my exemplar, is that he is always *present*. He'll pick one person out of crowd with whom to engage in deep conversation. He pays attention and asks the right questions. We think a lot alike. We're both analytical at the right times… logical…very positive in public…and we're both worriers – especially when it comes to our loved ones - to the point where some outsiders have called it "a Scott neurosis".

## Ithaquesian

The word *mentor* comes from Ithaca, Greece. Homer's Odyssey describes how Odysseus, king of Ithaca, left to go and fight in the Trojan War and entrusted his son, Telemachus, to Mentor, his faithful friend. Mentor was to teach Odysseus's son and to oversee the king's household. I love that my mentor, Uncle Merlin is an Ithaquesian. While my dad and his older brother were born in South Africa, Uncle Merlin was born in Ithaca.

I've often said to bosses of mine who have met Uncle Merlin, "If you have a problem with me, blame him. He taught me. He gave me the foundation on which to build".

# You Have To Want It

*I have been a seeker and I still am. But I stopped asking the books and the stars. I started listening to the teaching of my soul.*

—Rumi

**THERE IS MUCH** debate as to whether leaders are born or made. Perhaps it's a bit of both. I've observed that people who are not natural leaders cannot lead well, even with the best leadership training. However, those who are born to lead must be *willing* to lead.

I've always been a leader. Leaders do not conform and I've never conformed. Society's norm is often mediocre and most certainly never good enough for me, so I refuse to conform to it. From primary school onwards, I've always taken a leadership role. In my adult life, I've been a leader in my family, in my art of theatre, and in the workplace.

But my leadership development really began in earnest when I left my marriage to Horace Jones, for it was then that my career took off. I had to get out into the world of commerce and lead. By the time I was CEO of *United Business*

*Women* (UBW), I was a competent leader and able to evoke the best out of my people.

### ANONYMOUS PHONE CALL

It was 2009 and I was working at Telos and also working part-time at a global women's entrepreneurship organisation, when I received an anonymous phone call. Someone had sponsored me to attend an exclusive three-day workshop with an internationally well-known and respected leadership guru.

I was thrilled. I drove to the venue, a fully sustainable green conference center and hotel in the bush outside of Iliwa. The African bush always inspires me and I loved it.

I was one of twenty-five leaders selected to attend...an enormous privilege. I had read the guru's books and loved his philosophies. I was blessed!

Although I knew that I was an effective leader, I couldn't decipher what the guru was seeing in me as the sessions progressed. I participated in several exercises and, each time, my responses were quite different than those of the others. I was different. It was awkward. I felt off my mark...uncomfortable. I was extraordinary and I didn't like it. I didn't want to stand out. I was embarrassed.

### UNEASINESS OVER DINNER

The guru moved from table to table to interact personally with the participants. My turn came. He sat opposite me and I felt uneasy. The guru explained how unusual my style of leadership was and what my actions and option selections during our exercises meant. He referred to one particular exercise during which I had chosen one of the nine etchings by Dutch artist Jan Montyn that his guest lecturer, Willem HJ de Liefde, had presented. The etchings represented the Universal Life Cycle. Apparently, the etching I chose revealed that I had

---

been through the whole life cycle. Nobody else had chosen that one.

I fully understood what the guru was conveying...that I am a leader. That I should *allow* myself to take the lead. He knew that I was holding back. To this day, I don't know why I hold back. It could be my upbringing or the way I was socialised. The guru knew that I had the potential to be a great leader and this made me very uncomfortable.

### CORNERED

I avoided the guru for the remainder of the workshop in hopes of averting his piercing understanding of my leadership talent. He was touching on a sore point...*my calling*. My reluctance to lead was due neither to a lack of confidence nor fear. Simply put, I don't want to lead.

I've never had ambitions of being a leader, but it comes up time and time again. I have led well. I still do, particularly in the workplace. But I'd rather be led than have to lead. Towards the end of the three-day workshop, the guru cornered me.

"You need to stop tuning your instrument and play", he said.

I smiled, changed the subject, got in my car and left the workshop early. Yes, it was cowardly of me, but I was too uncomfortable.

As I exited the dirt road and got back onto the highway, I was listening to Radio 702. Radio 702 played Golden Oldies on Sundays and boasted that it never repeated the same song in one day. But, during the two-hour drive back to Iliwa, Neil Diamond's *Play Me* played *twice*.

*And so it was that I came to travel*

*Upon a road that was thorned and narrow*

*Another place, another grace*

*Would save me*

*You are the sun, I am the moon*

*You are the words, I am the tune*

*Play me*

*You are the sun, I am the moon*

*You are the words, I am the tune*

*Play me...*

I freaked out.

The guru's words echoed through my head. *You need to stop tuning your instrument and play.* A mighty battle waged within me for days. Is leadership a calling? Is this God speaking to me? Or is this a temptation to stand up and lead when I shouldn't?

I still don't have the answer.

# Twist And Jive

*Some days there won't be a song in your heart. Sing anyway.*

—Emory Austin

**MY ANTIDOTE TO** life's challenges, whether they be sadness, anxiety, ill health or even the loneliness of travelling the world alone, is to twist and jive!

Yes, twist and jive!

I love to dance. Music revives me. From classical, rap, reggae, pop and jazz, to Latin American and Gregorian chants, I love it all. Sometimes, I'm in the mood to listen only to instrumental music. However, when it's time to twist and jive, I hit the shuffle button on my iPod, iPhone, iPad or laptop and dance! I have music on all my devices.

I travel from low-key waltzes to vibrant Greek dance music, and then on to the blues, until I reach a gentle pan pipe melody, only to follow up by going wild to Elvis and London pub songs. Dancing lifts my soul and has kept me sane throughout the darkest times.

## THE GARDNER SISTERS

From the time I could walk, I could dance (or so my mom said). Dancing is in my blood. My paternal grandfather, Dennis Scott, had an Arthur-Murray-type dance studio where my beloved grandmother played the piano for each dance class. My grandfather also owned a movie house in Krugersdorp where my gran played the piano for the silent movies.

I began to dance formally at four years of age with the Gardner Sisters from Elangeni. The Gardner Sisters, who were very precise and strict, were quite legendary. When I was eight or nine, I loved to play outdoors and swim. I was very tanned, and the Gardner Sisters would rub calamine lotion on me and ask, "Have you ever seen a dark ballerina"? That was a dreadful thing to say to a child! It's just plain wrong. Thank goodness that stereotype has faded and there are now many exceptional ballerinas of colour, who are magnificent dancers.

## DISAPPOINTED IN DURBAN

I danced for many years and excelled. I still have many of the awards, medals, and certificates I earned passing my dance exams with honors and winning sections of the eisteddfods.

When my family moved from the Transvaal, which is now Gauteng, and on the plateau of South Africa, to Durban on the coast, the dance schools weren't of the same high calibre. The teacher in Durban refused to put me in with the sixteen year olds, even though I was dancing at their level. Rather, she advised my mother to switch me from ballet and tap to Spanish and modern dancing. And, as I was too young to insist on pursuing the ballet and tap I loved so much, I began to learn Spanish and modern dancing.

My time in Durban was quite melancholy. Before we moved to Durban, when I was dancing in Elangeni, I was either the winner or runner-up to Janet Marsh, a magnificent dancer, who ended up dancing for the Royal Ballet School in London. Oh, how I wished I had pursued my ballet! I would have been right there with her.

When I learned that we were moving back to Elangeni, I was overjoyed, even given that my dad had lost his business and I had lost my hair from the shock. I was excited to go back to the Transvaal and resume my dancing lessons with the Gardner Sisters. Tragically, this never happened.

Mom wanted me to wait until I was healthy and strong. She may have had other reasons, too. I wasn't privy to the financial situation. Months and months passed and still I did not go back to my study of dancing. But I never stopped dancing on my own. I danced in school plays. I took formal lessons for Greek dancing. And, if that were not enough, I would always *jeté* across the room at home. I kept my castanets close at hand and frequently burst into Spanish dance, too. But it wasn't until I was an adult that I took lessons again.

### No More Mourning

Horace Jones was a really good dancer and the dance floor was the one place where we moved together in perfect harmony. Once a week, we stepped out to dine and dance. Ah, we were a real showstopper. But, even with these weekly outings, I missed the discipline of learning the intricacies of new dances.

When my mother went home to be with our Lord, only two days before my divorce from Jones, I knew that in order to cope, I needed something to look forward to...something to distract me and help me stay physically fit for all that lay ahead. So I decided to take ballroom and Latin American dance lessons.

After my mother's passing, I did not observe the customary

Greek mourning period of forty days of wearing black, not attending any happy occasions, and one year of no joy, no dancing and no parties. I had just been through all of that for my father and his mourning period. I decided that I didn't care what society said. I didn't care what anybody said! I had to survive.

I registered at the local Fred Astaire Dance Studio. It was the best thing I ever did. The lessons were twice a week, with a social dance on Saturdays. I looked forward to it all. Dancing sustained me. It kept me fit and healthy, and it filled me with joy. I did exceedingly well and sped through my examinations. I also won prizes for my social dancing.

## STILETTOS

During a practice session in preparation for a very advanced exam, I pulled one foot very close to the other. My right stiletto heel went into the left foot shoe, and I went crashing to the ground, with my partner falling on top of my feet. I thought my foot was sprained, but later learned that it had been broken. Additionally, the right stiletto heal cut the underside of my left foot. It was a nightmare.

Over the next few days, I nursed the wound and wrapped the swollen and bruised ankle. But, months later on a trip to Europe with my best friend, Athena, I found myself in excruciating pain. I cut the trip short and headed home to South Africa to see an orthopedic surgeon. One plaster cast, a lot of prayer, sympathy and amazing support from my precious friend Wendy, and eight weeks later, my foot was completely healed.

My foot is absolutely perfect now and I continue to dance at every opportunity. Nine out of ten days, I have music flooding my home. The minute I'm slightly stressed, I press that shuffle button and I dance. It works!

# Triggers

*When I lose my temper, honey, you can't find it any place.*

—Ava Gardner

**WE ALL HAVE** triggers...those areas of heightened sensitivity to which we react fast and furiously. When someone pulls one of our triggers, it really is like a gun going off. Emotionally loud and dangerous. I have several triggers, but the one that takes my *moer*-meter from naught to one hundred in a nanosecond is when I witness abuse or injustice.

In 2010, I almost got arrested for reacting to a trigger. I had had a bumper bashing and was standing in the police station reporting the accident for insurance purposes, when a woman came running in crying and screaming, "The piece of paper the law gave me is not protecting me"! As the police were trying to calm her down, the story evolved that she had a restraining order against her husband because he had beaten her periodically and that she had just been beaten again. She was emphatic that the police needed to do something, because the restraining order was not enough to keep her safe.

The detective on duty kept repeating himself that there was nothing they could do because she has a restraining order and they couldn't get involved.

As you can imagine, and particularly with my own experience of having been physically, mentally, and verbally abused by my ex-husband, my heart went out to her immediately. I could not understand why the police weren't doing anything to help her. They had seen the bruises and the blood, yet they did nothing. She said, "I'm petrified to go home. He will kill me". But their answer remained the same. "There is nothing we can do. You have a restraining order". Unbelievable!

I opened my mouth and said a few things that I shouldn't have said. Very quickly, I realised that I was about to get into serious trouble. The officer on duty yelled, "Back off, lady! This is none of your business"! And it wasn't. But abuse is a trigger that, when pulled, makes it very difficult for me to regain my composure and control myself.

More recently, in a New York restaurant where tables are packed together and it's easy to overhear conversations, a woman at a table next to me was talking in a low whisper, but she might as well have been shouting. I heard every word she said. I wish I hadn't, because it was heartbreaking. The woman was demeaning her son, vomiting a continuous stream of vitriol aimed at the boy. The boy, who was about thirteen years old, was frightened. The woman went on and on and on and *on*, until the boy started to cry. As the boy became more and more distraught, her toxicity increased. Finally, she pulled out all the stops and launched a full assault on her son's character. The ugly injustice of the situation triggered me and I had to get up and leave, because I knew I was seconds away from speaking up and causing a very big scene.

Then in March of 2015, I was at a Consulate applying for a visa, when a woman in front of me, who was wearing a maid's uniform, was called up. Her young daughter was with her. Sound carried in the room and there was absolutely no privacy. The Consulate official questioning this woman asked her why she was seeking a visitor's visa for her daughter to travel to the USA. The woman very carefully explained that her daughter's father lives in the US and that the child was to visit her father over the school holidays. The Consulate representative responded by asking, "And are you certain that he is her father"?

My trigger did go off this time. I jumped up and glared at the Consulate representative and was about to let rip, when I remembered that I was in a government building and would be locked up if I said too much or, even, if I said anything they did not want to hear. I needed my work visa so I could return to New York to be with my son and, with a mighty struggle, I held my tongue. The representative's condescending; judgmental questioning of the woman continued until I couldn't bear to listen anymore and had to leave. I said to one of the women waiting, "I'm going to go to the bathroom. Please let me know if my number is called". And there I sat, in the bathroom, seething and trying to calm down.

Injustice, my most sensitive trigger…

# How Many Kettles?

*To me, if life boils down to one thing, it's movement.*
*To live is to keep moving.*

—Jerry Seinfeld

**I MOVED INTO** my apartment in Bay Ridge, Brooklyn, on a freezing cold December first. As I sat in my empty apartment waiting for the moving company to deliver my belongings from storage, I decided to unpack the boxes I had brought with me. Once I had unpacked them all, I sat and waited.

### A Cup of Tea
Still waiting for the movers, I wanted a cup of tea. I washed a tea cup and then realized I had no kettle! At that precise moment, the story of my life became a comic reality. I began to count how many kettles I had purchased over the years—these are the type of kettles with a heating element in them and that plug into an electrical outlet. I imagined a graph that measured the big adventures I've had in kettles. 2008 was kettles seven and eight, for example. Could the number of kettles one has possessed possibly be a measure

of how colourful, interesting or dramatic one's life has been? There certainly was a correlation between the kettles I've had and the big events in my life.

## THIRTEEN

As I sat there amongst the empty boxes, I took stock of each kettle I had bought. I thought about what was going on in my life at the time of the kettle changes. Thirteen kettles have come and gone, and I would have to buy number fourteen for my new home in Bayridge.

Now, out of the thirteen kettles, three were purchased for my son, Eric. One kettle when he returned to South Africa in 2008, which we gave to a dear friend of mine, Irene, when he moved back to the United States. She still has it and I'm thrilled to use it when I visit her in Cape Town.

Another kettle was purchased for Eric's man-cave when we shared a house in Brooklyn in 2011. When we packed up that house and I returned to live in South Africa, I gave that kettle away to my dear friends Roger and Cristina because South Africa has a different voltage. It still brings me great joy to sit down with them over a cup a tea made from that kettle. Cristina makes a good British cup of tea and we have shared many memorable and life-changing conversations over a cuppa.

The third kettle I bought for Eric was when he set up his new apartment in Manhattan in 2012. A coffee connoisseur, he actually didn't use the kettle at all until 2014 when his beloved fiancé, Ariel, taught him the delights of drinking tea.

This still leaves us with ten kettles. While not a single one ever broke down, I left them for various reasons…moving house, moving countries, getting divorced, given to people in need, and so on.

How dramatic has your life been, measured in kettles?

# Against All Odds

*You were born with potential.*
*You were born with goodness and trust.*
*You were born with ideals and dreams.*
*You were born with greatness.*
*You were born with wings.*
*You are not meant for crawling so don't.*
*You have wings.*

*Learn to use them and fly.*

—Rumi

**AS YOU RECALL,** the doctors did not expect Eric to survive, let alone thrive. But God is the Great Physician and I praise Him for His miracles. Eric's accomplishments as a grown man are all the sweeter for the bleak prognoses I received when he was an infant. I cannot look into my son's beautiful face without seeing the power and love of God for all His children. Eric is living proof that God answers our prayers.

The love and care that Eric has shown me, coupled with his many notable achievements, have completed my life. Eric is my greatest achievement.

My deepest desire for my child was that he would grow into a wonderful human being, healthy, enlightened and able to contribute to the betterment of humankind. Yes, I am fiercely proud of him. But with every one of his triumphs, humbleness and happiness overwhelm me.

Eric has been able to accomplish things that are mind-blowing. Anyone who uses excuses such as 'coming from a broken home' or 'not having financial support to start a career or go to university' should think again. Eric beat the odds against him every time. He beat ill health, the absence of a father, his mother's two divorces, the loss of his homes, witnessing his stepfather's emotional abuse of his mother... you get the picture. He overcame it all. He used the crises to drive him to effect positive change. He turned every test into a testimony and every mess into a message.

Whether it was the sports he played—from rugby to boxing, from professional paintball at international championships to Brazilian Jiu-Jitsu—or in his academic life, Eric has always excelled. His commitment and determination are exemplary. His awards, trophies, medals, diplomas and certifications are my pride and joy. More importantly though, it is his character of kindness, consideration, respect, warm-heartedness and caring, and his incredible sense of humour of which I am most proud.

# Dreams Do Come True

*Life is either a daring adventure or nothing at all.*

—Helen Keller

**AT THE TENDER** age of eleven, Eric fell in love with the United States of America. We had toured extensively and our last stop before returning to South Africa was New York City. He exclaimed atop the Empire State Building, "Mom, I am going to come and live in New York and I'm going to work in one of these very tall skyscrapers"!

"Of course, my son", I said, pleased that I had always taught him to dream BIG.

Not by the furthest stretch of my imagination did I think that Eric would be head-hunted to work in New York at One Penn Plaza, a 'very tall skyscraper' indeed and virtually next to the Empire State Building.

Eric's career has been an inspiration and continues to astound me and all who know him. He has won many awards in all the roles he has held to date including the all-significant peer awards. He continues to be invited to present and to teach at global conferences. His work has been published. He has been invited to comment on news events relative to his profession on live television several times. His effective training has been recorded by companies to train their employees. He is recognized as a subject expert world-wide.

When he told me in 2010 that his dream was to work on Wall Street, I encouraged him once again. Throughout his life, I have reminded him, "Dream BIG, my son". This time, I instinctively knew that it would only be a matter of time because, when Eric sets his mind on a goal, he achieves it. A year later, he was working for a company on Wall Street!

One of my most happy-tear-streaming-mommy-moments was when I saw his handsome face on the NASDAQ screen in Times Square, New York, as he opened up the stock markets in April 2014. That same year, Eric was selected to be part of a small team that would collaborate with the Department of Homeland Security to protect the financial markets as part of the President's directive that the markets be considered critical national infrastructure. At the end of the meeting in Washington, D.C., Eric was awarded a Challenge Coin. A Challenge Coin or medallion is one that bears an organization's insignia or emblem. Officials occasionally give them to non-military personnel for outstanding service or rewards. Eric, a civilian, received this significant coin as a symbol of appreciation and recognition for his profound contribution to the country.

More recently, my son's *philotimo* guided him when he needed to choose between prestige and comfort, or working for the good of humanity. He chose to work in a company that makes a positive impact in the world of cancer patients. He chose to use his God-given talents to make a difference for others.

I thank God for my Miracle Son…

My life…

My everything.

# End Of Act 1

*I want to be thoroughly used up when I die, for the harder I work, the more I love. I rejoice in life for its own sake. Life is no 'brief candle' for me. It is a sort of splendid torch which I've got a hold of for the moment, and I want to make it burn as brightly as possible before handing it on to future generations.*

—George Bernard Shaw

**EARLIER, I WROTE** of my love of theatre. My favorite monologue of all time, and the one for which I earned the highest marks in exams and eisteddfods, is an extract from Jean Anouilh's *Antigone*, an adaptation of Sophocles' 5<sup>th</sup> century BC play, *Antigone*. I had mastered the characterization of the young Antigone in this Greek tragedy. And so, Antigone's words echo through my mind often:

*"I want everything of life, I do; and I want it now! I want it total, complete: otherwise I reject it! I will not be moderate. I will not be satisfied with the bit of cake you offer me if I promise to be a good little girl. I want to be*

*sure of everything this very day; sure that everything will be as beautiful as when I was a little girl. If not, I want to die!"*

— Jean Anouilh, Antigone

Antigone's words have often whispered to me when I have had difficult decisions to make. Her words reverberated in my head when I had to blow the whistle. Her words resonated loudly like clanging cymbals when I knew I had to leave the father of my beloved son. The booming of her words ricocheted and would not be still when I knew I had to leave my abusive marriage. Antigone encouraged me never to settle for anything or anyone less than I deserve. After all, I am a child of the King of kings.

To this day, I hear Antigone's words. Never will I extinguish my burning desire to live life to the full.